LENIN

▣ ▣ ▣

This is a volume in a new series of PORTRAITS, devoted to figures who have changed the world we live in. The series is edited by Walter Kaufmann, Professor of Philosophy at Princeton University.

The first three volumes are:
    SARTRE *by Hazel E. Barnes*
    WITTGENSTEIN *by William Warren Bartley III*
    LENIN *by Rolf H. W. Theen*

They will soon be followed by:
    LUTHER *by Richard Marius*
    ENGELS *by Alfred Meyer*
    LINCOLN *by Hans Morgenthau*

Rolf H. W. Theen

LENIN

Genesis and Development
of a Revolutionary

回 回 回 回 回

J. B. LIPPINCOTT COMPANY
Philadelphia and New York

U.S. Library of Congress Cataloging in Publication Data

Theen, Rolf H. W., birth date
    Lenin: genesis and development of a revolutionary.

    (Portraits)
    Bibliography: p.
    1. Lenin, Vladimir Il'ich, 1870–1924.
I. Title.
DK254.L4T47   947.084'1'0924 [B]   73–1802
ISBN–0–397–00830–9

Meinen Eltern,
deren Opfern ich meine Erziehung verdanke

CONTENTS

回 回 回

If any man made history, Lenin did. But for him, Marxism would not be accepted now by one-third of mankind, and Marx himself might be remembered only as one of dozens of nineteenth-century intellectuals. Thus Lenin seems to have been the incarnate refutation of the Marxist view of history—and Marxism is in large measure a view of history. According to Marx, major historical developments are in some sense necessary and even predictable, and the presence of this or that individual here or there is not decisive. Such men as Lenin, and also Stalin and Hitler, suggest that Marx was wrong and that accidents play a crucial role in history. Moreover, Marx predicted that "the revolution" would occur in the advanced industrial societies of the West and not in Russia or China. One might therefore have expected Lenin to say, more or less: "You have heard that Marx said . . . But I say . . ." Instead, Lenin made Marxism the creed of millions.

Rolf Theen brings to life Lenin as a human being. He shows how Lenin gradually formed his own revolutionary world view and how he transformed Marxism. Theen is thoroughly at home both in Lenin's writings and in the multilingual literature about him and offers many new interpretations. In the notes, everything is documented meticulously, but the text can be read straight through and is never weighed down by the scholarship that backs it up. It is rare for a scholar in any field to be able to communicate so much excitement, and doubly rare for anyone to compress such a wealth of information into such a short book.

For those who want to find out what Lenin thought and did, this is a superb introduction. At the same time this book is also a genuine contribution to Lenin scholarship. Those who take a more worshipful view of Lenin will have to grapple with Theen's account.

WALTER KAUFMANN

An enumeration of the most influential men in the twentieth century would undoubtedly have to include Vladimir Ilyich Ulyanov-Lenin. Though not lacking in tragic components, his life is in many ways a success story unparalleled in the annals of modern history. Of relatively obscure social origin, born and raised in one of the provincial backwaters of Russia, Lenin was a recognized Marxist, political publicist, and revolutionary leader by the time he was thirty years old. At the age of forty-seven, he became the founder of the first Communist regime and the leader of a political movement which —within the short span of one generation—would succeed in establishing control over more than one-third of mankind and would aspire to extend that control to the rest of the world. Eminent historians such as Arnold Toynbee have ranked the Bolshevik leader with Einstein, Freud, and Hitler as one of the four men who gained world fame in our time and left their personal imprint on our age.

And, indeed, in many respects we live in a post-Lenin world. In Russia and China, the two Communist giants, as well as in the other Communist countries, the name of Lenin is invoked as the ultimate authority on virtually every aspect of human life and knowledge, in very much the same way religious believers in the past referred to the scriptures and sacred texts of their faith as the ultimate source of truth. According to Soviet figures, during 1918 to 1968 nearly 350 million copies of Lenin's writings were published in one hundred different languages in the USSR alone. Outside Russia, more than 4,000 editions of Lenin's works have been published in forty-eight countries in fifty-one different languages.[1] More important, throughout the world the name of Lenin and the political doctrine he created have come to symbolize the repudiation of the modern Western middle-class way of life—with the important exception of science and technology.

Himself the heir of a long, fascinating and rich revolutionary tradition, Lenin also became the recipient of a ready-made revolutionary doctrine from the West, namely, Marxism. The fusion of Western Marxism, elements of the Russian revolutionary tradition, and Lenin's own peculiar psychology resulted in the formulation of a revolutionary doctrine that—in conjunction with objective historical forces—resulted not only in the October Revolution of 1917, but also in the inspiration of various political movements opposed to liberal democracy throughout the world.

While the literature on Lenin has grown to truly stupendous proportions—the books that have been written on Lenin in the USSR alone would fill a sizable library—relatively little attention has been given to the formative stage of Lenin's development as a revolutionary and political thinker. With the exception of the brilliant but dated biography of the young Lenin by Leon Trotsky, recently published in English translation,[2] the excellent study of the intellectual evolution of the young Lenin by Richard Pipes,[3] the fragment of what was to have been a major biography of the Bolshevik leader by Isaac Deutscher,[4] and the research into Lenin's early years by Nikolai Valentinov,[5] most biographies of the founder of the Soviet state neglect his childhood, youth and adolescence. At the same time, important collections of documentary materials, correspondence, and memoirs published in the Soviet Union in recent years at last make possible a more detailed and thorough examination of Lenin's early years.

The present volume is a study of the development of Lenin as a revolutionary. Its main focus is on the years 1887 to 1900, the period in Lenin's life during which he worked out his revolutionary *Weltanschauung,* eventually placing himself at the center of the revolutionary universe. However, the story has also been briefly carried forward to 1924, the year of Lenin's death. Throughout this study the emphasis has been on Lenin—the man, revolutionary, theoretician, and political leader. Given the space limitations of this volume, a great deal of peripheral history, interesting and significant though it may be, had to be neglected.

I have used the third edition of Lenin's collected works in Russian (published concurrently with the second edition) as well as the more recent and complete fifth edition. Unless otherwise indicated, all references to Lenin's writings are to the fifth edition. Russian names and words commonly found in English literature have been rendered in the text in accordance with their accepted English orthography. Less well known Russian names and words I have transliterated, using a modified version of the Library of Congress system (omitting ligatures and diacritical marks).

In order to avoid a confusion of dates with other sources, I have listed the most important dates according to both the Julian calendar, which Russia used until February 14, 1918, and the Western (Gregorian) calendar. The Julian calendar was twelve days behind the Gregorian calendar in the nineteenth century and thirteen days behind in the twentieth century; thus, for instance, the Bolshevik seizure of power in Petrograd took place on October 25, 1917, according to the Russian calendar, but on November 7, 1917, according to the Western calendar. Less important dates before February 1 (14), 1918, conform to the Julian calendar then in force in Russia; dates after February 1 (14), 1918, conform to the Gregorian calendar.

I have been interested in the study of Lenin for a number of years. The publication of this volume, which attempts to summarize part of my research on the Bolshevik leader, gives me a welcome opportunity to express my deep gratitude to the individuals and institutions that in various ways have assisted and encouraged my research over the years, in particular: Anna Burgina, Boris Sapir, Peter Scheibert, Bertram D. Wolfe, and the late Boris I. Nicolaevsky; the Hoover Institution on War, Revolution and Peace; the International Institute for Social History, Amsterdam; the Lenin State Library, Moscow; the Library of Congress; the New York Public Library; the following university libraries: California (Berkeley), Chicago, Columbia, Harvard, Illinois, Indiana, Stanford, and Yale. A special word of appreciation goes to Mrs. Cheryl Knodle and her staff of the Inter-Library Loan Department of the Purdue University Library for their splendid cooperation and efficiency in tracking down elusive sources in a strange language, and to Myron Q. Hale, Chairman of the Department of Political Science at Purdue University, for arranging to reduce my teaching obligations during the fall semester of 1971 and for his encouragement and support.

I owe a special debt of gratitude to Robert C. Tucker, Robert F. Byrnes, and Darrell P. Hammer for first stimulating my interest in Marxism, Lenin, and the

Russian revolutionary tradition as well as for valuable suggestions, comments, and constructive criticism of the manuscript, and to Walter Kaufmann for invaluable and sensitive editorial assistance. I am also indebted to Richard M. Haywood and to my colleagues, especially Robert Melson, James A. Stegenga, and Frank L. Wilson, for reading and criticizing the original manuscript, and to Edward L. Burlingame and Mrs. Hilda M. Rogers of J. B. Lippincott Company for their critical comments and editorial assistance. The responsibility for any errors of fact or interpretation, of course, rests solely with me.

My research was supported, at various times, by research and travel grants from the American Philosophical Society, the Inter-University Committee on Travel Grants, Iowa State University, the Joint Committee on Slavic Studies of the American Council of Learned Societies and the Social Science Research Council, and the Purdue Research Foundation. To all these institutions and organizations I want to express my gratitude and appreciation.

Finally, my greatest debt is to Norma and Tanya, who sacrificed a family vacation and the countless hours during which I wrestled with Lenin, and who in so many ways helped to make this book possible.

ROLF H. W. THEEN

Purdue University
September 1972

Revolution does not always come when things are going from bad to worse. . . . The regime that is destroyed by a revolution is almost always better than the one preceding it, and experience teaches us that usually the most dangerous time for a bad government is when it attempts to reform itself.

—Alexis de Tocqueville

[The problem is that] revolutions require a *passive* element, a *material* basis. Theory will be realized in a people only to the extent that it fulfills the needs of the people. . . . Will the theoretical needs be immediately practical needs? It is not enough that thought should seek to realize itself; reality must also strive toward thought.

—Karl Marx

The worst possible fate that can befall the leader of an extreme party is to be compelled to take over the government in an epoch when the movement is not yet ripe for the domination of the class which he represents, and for the realization of the measures which the domination of that class requires. . . . Thus he inevitably finds himself in an inextricable dilemma: What he *can* do contradicts his whole previous position, his principles, and the immediate interests of his party; and what he *ought* to do cannot be done. . . . Whoever finds himself in this precarious situation is irrevocably doomed.

—Friedrich Engels

Give us an organization of revolutionaries, and we shall overturn the whole of Russia.

—V. I. Lenin

No single man makes history. History cannot be seen, just as one cannot see grass growing. Wars and revolutions, kings and Robespierres, are history's organic agents, its yeast. But revolutions are made by fanatical men of action with one-track minds, geniuses in their ability to confine themselves to a limited field. They overturn the old order in a few hours or days, the whole upheaval takes a few weeks or at most years, but the fanatical spirit that inspired the upheavals is worshipped for decades thereafter, for centuries.

—Boris Pasternak

1
FAMILY, CHILDHOOD, AND YOUTH

When Ilya Nikolaevich Ulyanov and his wife, Maria, had their second son baptized in the spring of 1870 in the tiny Saint Nicholas Church in Simbirsk and gave him the name Vladimir, they little suspected that within a few decades he would become the founder of a new type of state and the leader of a movement whose political objectives coincided with the literal meaning and exhortation of his name, i.e., "rule the world" (*Vladi mir*). Nor did they anticipate that their son, the future Lenin, in his attempt to forcibly introduce communism in Russia, was destined to emulate the role of his historic namesake, Saint Vladimir, who in the tenth century had converted Russia to Eastern Orthodox Christianity, thus laying the foundation for a historical development that was to set Russia apart from the West. As a matter of fact, there was nothing in the circumstances surrounding Vladimir Ilyich Ulyanov's birth, ancestry or childhood which would have presaged his future role as a revolutionary and political leader.

Vladimir Ilyich Ulyanov became a figure of world historical significance under the name of Lenin—a pen name which he first used in a letter he wrote G. V. Plekhanov in January 1901 and adopted in public in December of that year, but which gained general acceptance, even among the members of his own party, only after 1903. In spite of the fact that he was known to the world primarily by this pseudonym, Lenin never abandoned his family name; he used it in private and official correspondence throughout his life. Even after 1917, as Chairman of the Council of People's Commissars, he preferred to sign government decrees and other documents with his family name, Vladimir Ulyanov, frequently adding Lenin in parentheses and usually abbreviating his first name, i.e., V. I. Ulyanov (Lenin).

The origin of the pseudonym "Lenin" has not been established. Lenin's relatives apparently were unable to shed light on this question. Some writers have suggested that it is derived from Lena, the name of a Gymnasium classmate. It is more likely, however, that Vladimir Ulyanov followed the example of his onetime idol and teacher G. V. Plekhanov and chose a pseudonym derived from the name of one of the great Russian rivers. Since Plekhanov had already preempted the name "Volgin" (after the Volga River), the eyes and mind of the thirty-one-year-old Vladimir Ulyanov turned farther east to the Lena, one of the great Siberian rivers. If the origin of the name "Lenin" can, indeed, be explained in this way, there is a certain symbolic and portentous significance in the choice of this pseudonym. For Plekhanov and Lenin were destined to become representatives of two different orientations within the Russian Marxist movement. Like the Volga and Lena Rivers in the vast Russian subcontinent, they came to personify the Western and Eastern poles of Russian Marxism. Sharing a common source and outlook at one time, their political views eventually diverged and grew increasingly farther apart. And like the two mighty Russian rivers, the impact of their political ideas and activity ultimately pointed in different directions.

It is possible, however, that the name "Lenin" was chosen purely accidentally and carries no special meaning or significance. Following the example of his contemporaries in the Russian revolutionary movement, Vladimir Ulyanov used numerous pseudonyms to conceal his identity from the czarist police—V. Frei, V. Ilin, K. Tulin, to mention only a few. Certainly it would be difficult, if not impossible, to find a logical or meaningful explanation for all the pseudonyms—a total of more than 150—which Lenin employed at one time or another during his life. In any case, only one of them is known throughout the civilized world today. It was under the name of Lenin that Vladimir Ulyanov made a lasting imprint on our age, becoming a historical figure whose shadow still falls authoritatively across the pages of modern history, not only influencing the present but also reaching into the future.[1] *

Ancestral Background

Lenin's father, Ilya Nikolaevich Ulyanov, was the youngest son of Nikolai Vasilievich Ulyanov, a poor tailor whose family background is uncertain,[2] and Anna Alekseevna Smirnova, the illiterate daughter of a Kalmyk. The paternal grandparents of the future Bolshevik leader were probably former serfs, who scratched out a meager existence in Astrakhan, a city at the mouth of the Volga. The Ulyanovs married late in life and in the 1830s, when Ilya Nikolaevich was born, were still uncertain about the correct spelling of the family name— a fact which suggests that Nikolai Vasilievich Ulyanov had only recently emerged from the obscurity of the peasant masses and acquired an identity of his own.[3] It was not until 1835, shortly before his death, that Lenin's grandfather, at the age of seventy, was granted official

* Superior numbers refer to the section of Notes at the end of the text.

status as a *meshchanin*[4]—a town dweller—and thus became a recognized citizen of Astrakhan.

Thanks to the self-sacrifice of his elder brother, Vasilii, who became the head of the family after the death of their father in 1838, and the support of a certain Nikolai Livanov, an archpriest in a neighboring parish and his godfather, Ilya Nikolaevich was able to obtain an education. He attended the local Gymnasium and in 1850 was graduated with honors, becoming the recipient of the first silver medal awarded in the almost fifty-year history of the school. His graduation certificate, however, explicitly barred him from entry into the civil service because of his social origin.[5] With the personal support of the director of the Astrakhan Gymnasium, he became the first graduate of that school to be admitted to Kazan University, at that time the only university in the eastern districts (*gubernii*) of Russia. His application for a scholarship having been rejected because of his low social status—his descent from the *meshchanskoe soslovie*—Ilya Nikolaevich was once again dependent on the support of his brother and his own ability to earn money as a tutor and private teacher. His diligence and dedication to his studies soon caught the attention of N. I. Lobachevsky, the famous mathematician and pioneer of non-Euclidean geometry, who—although already retired—took a personal interest in the promising student and, after Ilya's graduation from the Faculty of Mathematics and Physics in 1854, was instrumental in obtaining for him a position as senior teacher of physics and mathematics at the *Dvorianskii institut*—the Institute for the Nobility—in Penza. It was here, in the home of another schoolteacher, that Ilya Ulyanov met Maria Aleksandrovna Blank, the future mother of Lenin, whom he married in the summer of 1863.

If the paternal ancestry of Lenin creates problems for Soviet hagiography—which calls for pure Great Russian descent and anything but the startlingly successful career of his father, who eventually acquired a relatively high social status and became a member of the hereditary nobility—the ancestry of his mother poses an even greater dilemma: Lenin's maternal ancestors were definitely not of "proletarian" origin; what is more, on his mother's side, Lenin's lineage points to German, Swedish, and possibly Jewish, descent.

Lenin's mother (1835–1916) was the daughter of Dr. Alexander Dmitrievich Blank, a physician who practiced medicine in Saint Petersburg as well as in the *gubernii* of Smolensk, Perm, and Kazan. Lenin's sister Maria described him as "a progressive individual, interested in ideas, strong and independent, opposed to careerism and servility in any form." [6] On his retirement he purchased a small estate called Kokushkino (988 acres, after 1861 741 acres) in the *guberniia* of Kazan, where Lenin would spend many happy hours during his youth and "go into exile" after his expulsion from Kazan University. The family background of Dr. Blank has not been definitely established; the available evidence suggests that he came from a Russified German family or was a descendant of a Jewish merchant family from Odessa.[7]

Lenin's maternal grandmother was Anna "Ivanovna" Grosschopf, the daughter of Johann Gottlieb Grosschopf, a German merchant from Lübeck who in 1790 emigrated to Saint Petersburg and there married Anna Beata (Karlovna) Öhrstedt (also Östedt), the daughter of a Swedish goldsmith from Uppsala. As director of the firm of Ch. R. Schade, J. G. Grosschopf became a successful and prosperous citizen of the Russian capital, owning a large home in one of its fashionable districts, with a large library and a violin collection. His sons were equally successful: Karl Grosschopf became privy councilor and vice director of the Department of Foreign Trade; Gustav Grosschopf became director of customs in Riga, state councilor, and the owner of an estate in Lithuania; a third son became an officer. In other words, Lenin's maternal grandmother came from a cultured and well-to-do family. And in all probability it was the financial wealth of her family which enabled Dr. Blank to retire from his varied and sporadic career in medicine at the age of forty-five. When in 1847, after the death of his wife, Lenin's grandfather joined the ranks of the landed nobility in Kazan *guberniia* and became a serf-owning landlord—a *pomeshchik*—at Kokushkino, he brought with him Katerina Ivanovna Essen, his sister-in-law, to manage the household and bring up his five daughters. It is to this "strict aunt" that Lenin's mother largely owed her excellent, if informal, education and her cultivated mind—personal attributes which played a significant role in the upbringing of the Ulyanov children.[8]

The ancestral background of Lenin thus ranged from former serfs in the Volga region of Russia to members of the *haute bourgeoisie* in Germany; it spanned two continents and encompassed several religions and nationalities; it fused family backgrounds which, socially and culturally, must have been poles apart. Does this fact in any way detract from Lenin's stature as a historical figure or make him less Russian? On the contrary! Lenin was, as Louis Fischer has put it, "a child of Russia . . . and the fruit of a tree with long roots in her varied soil . . . a bridge between East and West, partaking of both yet struggling to be neither." [9]

Nevertheless, the full facts of Lenin's ancestry—

although essentially known since the 1930s, when Marietta Shaginian, a Soviet writer of Armenian origin, stumbled on archive data about Lenin's forebears in her research for a novel about the Ulyanov family—have never been allowed to enter into the vast biographical literature on Lenin published in the Soviet Union, the country which owes its present political and social physiognomy largely to "the scion of the landed gentry" (*"pomeshchich'e ditia"*) from Simbirsk, as Lenin once described himself.[10] The most recent official biography of the Bolshevik leader, published by the Institute of Marxism-Leninism in Moscow, an organization directly attached to the Central Committee of the Communist Party of the Soviet Union (CPSU), devotes less than ten words to his ancestry—and this in a country where patronymics have been a tradition for centuries and where it has been customary not only to register births and deaths, but also to make baptism, school enrollment and change of residence a matter of public record, a country where even today one of the first questions asked concerns one's family background.[11] Accurate and complete information about Lenin's ancestry has been systematically suppressed or overlooked because it does not fit into the carefully projected official image of the founder of Bolshevism—because it would reveal that Lenin did not come "from the people" or from a low social origin, facts which Lenin himself never hesitated to admit.

The Ulyanov Family

In the fall of 1863, shortly after their marriage, the Ulyanovs left Penza and moved to Nizhni Novgorod, at that time one of the most desirable and civilized cities on the Volga, with its own theater, lively intellectual circles, and an annual fair famous throughout Russia. The Gymnasium there was headed by A. V. Timofeev, who had been Ilya Ulyanov's teacher in Astrakhan and later one of his colleagues at the Institute for the Nobility in Penza. It was through his assistance that Lenin's father obtained a position as senior teacher of physics and mathematics—a position he held for six years. The Ulyanovs apparently found the atmosphere in Nizhni Novgorod very congenial: they became popular among the teachers and were socially active, and in later years they were to recall their life there with nostalgia.

A year after their move to Nizhni Novgorod, their first daughter, Anna (1864–1935), was born; two years later she was followed by their first son, Alexander (1866–87), affectionately called Sasha. In 1869 Ilya Nikolaevich was appointed Inspector of Public Schools for the *guberniia* of Simbirsk, and in September of that year, when Maria Aleksandrovna was expecting her third child, the Ulyanovs moved to another city on the Volga: Simbirsk (renamed Ulyanovsk in Lenin's honor after his death in 1924), then a city of 50,000. It was here in Simbirsk, on April 10 (22), 1870, that Vladimir Ilyich Ulyanov, the future Lenin, was born. He was followed by Olga (1871–91), Dimitri (1874–1943), and Maria (1878–1937), affectionately called Maniasha.[12]

Compared to colorful Nizhni Novgorod, historically a stronghold of the Russian merchant class, Simbirsk was dull and backward, a caste-ridden "nest of gentlefolk," a city over which "lay the torpidity of peace, the calm on land which is found at sea," as Goncharov described it in his novel *The Precipice* (1870). It was life in Simbirsk during the 1850s which inspired the same author to create a new literary type, Oblomov, in a novel by that name published in 1859. Goncharov's famous hero symbolized apathy, sluggishness and inactivity, idleness and fruitless daydreaming—the peculiar malaise that afflicted Russian society for so long. Twenty-one years to the month after the publication of *Oblomov's Dream,* an early extract of Goncharov's best-known novel, Simbirsk became the birthplace of the man who was destined to wake Russia forever from her Oblomovian slumber.

In many respects, the quality of life decreased for the Ulyanov family when they moved to Simbirsk. There is evidence that Lenin's mother had difficulty adjusting to her new environment and life in the provincial capital.[13] And Lenin's brother Alexander, as a twenty-year-old, was terrified by the prospect of having to return to Simbirsk: "There one could grow completely dull. No books, no people." [14]

As a *meshchanin* and descendant of a non-Russian nationality, married to a "foreigner," Ilya Ulyanov did not fit easily into the existing pattern of the social hierarchy in Simbirsk, in spite of his position. Unlike his wife, however, he was much too busy and preoccupied with his work to let this fact bother him; he had neither the time nor the inclination to try to overcome the barriers which separated his family from local society. Working tirelessly from morning till night, he threw himself into his new work, which involved administration rather than teaching. He was in charge of building schools, training teachers, and promoting education in a vast *guberniia* with virtually no roads and nearly a million peasants scattered over thousands of villages. Having himself advanced from humble social origins the hard way, Lenin's father firmly believed in education as the only effective instrument of social progress. He was an enthusiastic supporter of the Great Reforms and worked diligently to make use of the opportunities which they opened up in the field of education. Unpretentious and modest in his conduct and life-style, firm but sympathetic and understanding toward his subordinates, constantly experimenting with new ideas in education, he became an extremely successful, dedicated, and well-liked civil servant—the very opposite of the typical czarist *chinovnik* satirized so trenchantly in the works of Gogol and other Russian writers.[15] Throughout his life, he remained a devout Greek Orthodox and a loyal subject of the czar. In 1874 he was promoted to the position of Director of Public Schools and received the rank of Actual Councilor of State—a rank which, among other advantages, involved the status of hereditary nobility.[16]

Lenin's mother, too, was a remarkable individual. Although she had never received a formal education, she was well read in history and literature, interested in music, and knew English and French, in addition to German and Russian, the languages in which she was brought up. She was gracious, even-tempered and of strong character, a person of cheerful disposition, totally devoted to her family and to the upbringing and education of her children. Never raising her voice and rarely resorting to punishment, Maria Aleksandrovna was patient but firm with her children.[17] She played games with them and worked with them, helped them with their homework and with various projects such as the "publication" of a weekly handwritten magazine on which all the Ulyanov children collaborated. She ran an exemplary household, was industrious and efficient, and had a penchant for neatness and orderliness. According to Nadezhda K. Krupskaya, Lenin's wife, who knew Maria Aleksandrovna well, Lenin owed his organizational ability, which was to become one of his most important political assets, to his mother.[18]

The Ulyanov children varied considerably in regard to interests, character, temperament and disposition; yet Maria Ulyanova seems to have had a close and intimate relationship with all of them. Without exception, all her children loved her deeply and held her in the highest esteem. This suggests that Lenin's mother must have had the rare ability to treat and understand each of her children as an individual. Her bearing during periods of great crisis—the sudden death of her husband in 1886 and the execution of her oldest son in 1887—testify to her exceptional strength of character. If these tragic events broke her spirit, she succeeded in concealing this fact from her children. Even during periods of grief and adversity she placed her children above herself, providing for them material comfort, giving them love and security. No wonder that Lenin, whose dedication to the cause of revolution eventually eclipsed and crowded out virtually all personal feelings and emotions, always preserved a very close and special relationship to his mother and regarded her as a "saint." [19] The day after his return to Russia in April of 1917, at a time of turbulent events and pressing duties, he went to the Volkovo cemetery in Saint Petersburg and prostrated himself on her grave.

There is no doubt that the Ulyanovs were, in many respects, an exceptionally closely knit family. Even after Maria Aleksandrovna's children had grown up, they kept in close contact with her and with each other by means of an extensive correspondence.[20] Yet the picture of a perfectly harmonious family life presented in Soviet accounts of the Ulyanovs—with the notable exception of Shaginian—is probably considerably overdrawn.

To begin with, there were certain differences between the parents in outlook and temperament—differences which the children must have sensed and felt. Their father had been raised in the Greek Orthodox faith and was devoutly religious; their mother had been brought up by a Lutheran aunt and "did not like to go to church." While religious rites and ceremonies were observed in Lenin's home and the Ulyanovs regularly celebrated what Pushkin called "the customs of dear ancientry," it was only Ilya Nikolaevich who retained a deep religious faith until the end of his life.[21] Lenin's mother apparently was not a religious person. Whether her indifference to religion was due to skepticism or apathy, we do not know; perhaps she could never get used to the ritual of the Russian Orthodox Church. In any case, only at times of extreme stress and despair is she reported to have turned to prayer. The Ulyanov children were allowed to decide for themselves in matters of religious faith. When Alexander told his father one day that he would no longer attend church, Ilya Nikolaevich accepted the decision his son had made and the issue was not raised again.[22] Lenin, according to his own testimony, ceased to believe in God at the age of sixteen.[23] Thus there is no evidence that the matter of religion ever became a major issue in the Ulyanov home. Nevertheless, the difference in the religious outlook of the parents probably resulted in an undercurrent of tension in the Ulyanov family of which the children were aware.[24]

Furthermore, given Maria Aleksandrovna's varied intellectual and cultural interests, she must have felt deprived and unfulfilled when after their move to Simbirsk—owing to her husband's frequent absences from home for weeks and even months at a time—she found herself without anyone to talk to but her children and

Varvara Grigor'evna Sarabatova, a peasant woman whom the Ulyanovs had hired as a nurse. While Ilya Nikolaevich was very much involved with his environment outside the family, the life of his wife centered almost exclusively on the upbringing of the children. It seems likely that the pronounced differences in their respective roles and activities constituted a source of tension between the parents. Moreover, the frequent prolonged absences of the father must have had an unsettling effect on the emotional development of the children.[25] A recent study attempting to explain the attributes of the revolutionary personality in terms of psychoanalytical theory has emphasized the pattern of antipaternal rebellion as an important dimension in the lives of both Lenin and his brother Alexander.[26]

Finally, there is no reason to believe that the Ulyanov family was exempt from the kind of sibling rivalry which is found in most families. There is a great deal of evidence that the Ulyanov children grew up in a very competitive atmosphere, both at home and at school. They liked races of all kinds and other competitive games. Beginning at the age of eight or nine, Lenin played chess with his father and Sasha, and later with Olga and Dimitri. When Lenin was graduated from the Gymnasium in 1887 at the top of his class and received the coveted gold medal in recognition of his academic performance, he was merely continuing a "family tradition." Both Anna and Sasha had received the same distinction.

Apparently Sasha was the favorite of the younger children and occupied a special position within the family; he also had a very close and special relationship to Anna, as is apparent from her memoirs. Although Lenin tried to emulate his older brother "to the point of triviality," he was not very close to him. In fact, there is considerable evidence that the two brothers differed greatly in their interests, habits, and temperament. According to Anna, the Ulyanov children "paired" by age: she was closest to Sasha, who was two years younger; Lenin's closest playmate was Olga, one year his junior; finally, Dimitri and Maria, four years apart, were playmates.

Thus the Ulyanovs seem to have been a rather typical family. Both Maria Aleksandrovna and Ilya Nikolaevich were devoted parents; they encouraged discipline, industry and diligence, especially in schoolwork, but they also allowed their children considerable freedom to develop their own ideas and values. All the Ulyanov children became excellent students. "We lived in easy circumstances," Lenin himself was to tell one of his comrades in 1904. "We did not know hunger or cold; we were surrounded by all sorts of cultural opportunities and stimuli, books, music, and diversions." [27] The fragmentary evidence suggests that the Ulyanov family was not immune to the normal pressures and tensions which characterize all complex human relationships. Nevertheless, while the picture of a perfectly harmonious family life presented in Soviet biographies of Lenin is exaggerated, there is no reason to doubt the words of Anna that "the childhood of Vladimir Ilyich and his brothers and sisters was cloudless and happy." [28]

Vladimir Ilyich Ulyanov

Unlike his two brothers, Vladimir Ulyanov strongly resembled his father. As an adult, he had the same large, prominent forehead (described as "Socratic" by Maxim Gorky), a feature which was accentuated by his early baldness; the same small, piercing, hazel eyes, slightly slanted; and the same prominent cheekbones. Gorky was to write about Lenin's "Mongolian type," and Western biographical literature abounds with descriptions of Lenin's "Asiatic" appearance. Lenin himself, apparently, was fully aware of his distinctive features. When in the fall of 1917 he was forced to leave Russia and tried to cross the border in the disguise of a fireman on a Finnish locomotive, he realized that even the wig he was wearing could not conceal the Mongolian features of his face. Bursting into laughter, he replied to the question of a startled Finnish worker, who had helped him with his disguise: "But my eyes are a little slanted." [29]

Much has been made of Lenin's "Asiatic" heritage. Some writers have even tried to link the excesses of the Russian Revolution to the "Mongolian" features of its leader. Thus, in the case of Lenin, even his outward appearance, which surely ought to be a man's least controversial aspect, has been used to create or reinforce prejudices and to serve political purposes. As a matter of fact, however, the Mongolian or Oriental features which we find in Lenin were quite common among the Great Russians of his time and can be observed in millions of Russians today.[30] If anything, Lenin's physical appearance was typical because it reflected the process of the intermingling of races which had been going on for centuries in Russia—especially in the Volga region. The average Russian today is usually unaware of the Mongolian traits in his fellow countrymen. And Valentinov tells us that most of the people around Lenin never gave a thought to his Asiatic appearance. The fact is that these physical characteristics tend to be more easily discerned by the Western eye, which has remained more sensitive to them.

The earliest available photograph of Lenin shows

him when he was four years old, together with his sister Olga. Young Lenin, who was affectionately called Volodia or Voloden'ka, has his left arm around his sister; he is dressed in a light-colored shirt held together—in Russian fashion—by a belt, wide trousers, and black boots. He has curly blond hair; his full face is charming and friendly, with a soft, winning smile. He would have been the pride of any mother.

A photograph of the Ulyanov family taken in 1879, when Lenin was nine years old, shows him sitting next to his father, his right arm on his father's knee. Young Vladimir is dressed in the gala uniform worn by students of the Gymnasium. His face is no longer full and produces an almost triangular effect. The expression is more serious; the growing resemblance to his father is striking.

A photograph of Lenin taken in 1887, at the time of his graduation from the Gymnasium in Simbirsk, shows a carefully groomed young man, with full lips and a very handsome, intelligent and energetic face. It is an attractive and serious face, which expresses determination and self-confidence.

As Trotsky has pointed out, Lenin in no way resembled the classical stereotype of the Russian nihilist. He kept his hair trimmed and his clothes neat. In fact, in many respects he was a model child and son. As a youngster he became the favorite of Varvara Grigor'evna, the nurse in the Ulyanov home. "These other children are good—they are gold," she would say, "but my Voloden'ka is a diamond." [31] He apparently was an imaginative, if somewhat domineering and noisy, playmate. Because of his bulky frame and short stature, the children called him "Kubyshkin," i.e., "the bellied jug." He liked to break his toys rather than to play with them. Sometimes he played so loudly that he disturbed the rest of the family and kept the other children from getting their schoolwork done. Whenever this happened, he would be made to sit in the "black chair" in his father's study until he was ready to behave himself. Whether this actually constituted punishment for young Lenin is doubtful: usually he fell promptly asleep.

All the accounts of Lenin's youth suggest that he was a very energetic and active youngster. During the summer, which the Ulyanov family—falling into the rhythm of the life of the Russian nobility—regularly spent in the country on the Kokushkino estate, Volodia would take the lead in inventing all sorts of games. He apparently saw no danger or hostility in his environment. Having become an excellent swimmer and a rower of great endurance, he tried fearlessly to master the most treacherous crosscurrents of the Sviyaga and Volga, and took long trips in his boat. Once or twice he had to be pulled out of the water.

In some ways, young Lenin's behavior at home stood in marked contrast to his conduct at school. Among the members of his family, he is reported to have been quick-tempered, impatient, extremely proud and self-confident. In her memoirs, Lenin's sister Anna comments on his adolescent stage, recalling the harshness of his speech, his rudeness and arrogance, as well as his strong tendency to mock—qualities which disturbed her and especially Alexander. These negative characteristics and a growing impertinence were particularly noticeable after the death of Ilya Nikolaevich in 1886. However, after the execution of Alexander a year later, they gradually disappeared. As he grew more mature, Lenin apparently also overcame his quick temper—a change which Anna Ulyanova attributes to the influence of Sasha.[32]

Like the other Ulyanov children, Vladimir was at

first tutored by private teachers at home. At the age of nine he entered the classical Gymnasium in Simbirsk, where he became not only the top student in his class but also a model of good behavior. He earned the respect and admiration of his teachers, including F. M. Kerensky, the director of the school, who taught literature in the advanced classes and—such are the capricious ways of history—was the father of Alexander Kerensky, whose government Lenin was destined to overthrow in 1917. A rather conservative liberal like Ilya Nikolaevich and a close friend of the family, Kerensky-père did not desert the Ulyanovs after the arrest and execution of Sasha. On the contrary, he used his position and influence to secure admission of his star pupil to Kazan University in 1887, being convinced that he had the makings of a great classical scholar.

In his certificate of maturity, for which he qualified at the age of seventeen, Lenin received the grade of five —the highest possible mark—in all his subjects, except in logic. He showed a strong preference for the humanities; his favorite subjects were Latin, Greek, Russian literature, history, and geography. Years later he told Krupskaya that Latin was one of the "dangerous addictions"—the others were literature, music, and chess!— from which he had to free himself before he could become a revolutionary. His attentiveness, industry, and conduct were judged "excellent." [33] The only negative aspect in this picture is the fact that Vladimir Ulyanov —while not completely isolated from his schoolmates —did not have any close friends among them. Kerensky remarked about his "excessive reserve," his "tendency to withdraw," and his "generally unsociable attitude" when he recommended him for admission to the final examination.[34]

Soviet biographers of Lenin have frequently attempted to make Vladimir Ulyanov into a child prodigy of a revolutionary. The facts speak against such a portrayal. While there are indications that after the death of his father the star pupil of the Simbirsk Gymnasium began to throw off authority—he abandoned religion, increasingly often showed disrespect to his mother, and started to criticize the school authorities—there is no reason to attribute a deeper significance to these actions, to see in them more than the kind of adolescent rebellion which for many young people is an integral part of their quest for adulthood, without necessarily resulting in the development of a revolutionary *Weltanschauung*. The available evidence suggests that during his Gymnasium years Vladimir Ulyanov was in every respect a model student, who showed no sign of a revolutionary orientation. On the contrary, he seemed to be in perfect harmony with his environment. His behavior at school did not display the recklessness, rudeness, and arrogance which occasionally surfaced in his conduct at home. There were no reports of impertinence or insubordination. This "exceedingly talented, always diligent and conscientious" young man, as Kerensky characterized him shortly before his graduation, had successfully completed the first important step toward what promised to be a brilliant academic or professional career. He had not yet developed an interest in sociopolitical questions. He was still "addicted" to literature, in particular Turgenev, whose works he read and reread. In short, Vladimir Ulyanov had not yet become Lenin.

When in the summer of 1886 Alexander Ulyanov returned from Saint Petersburg University to spend the summer with his family on the Kokushkino estate, he brought with him several books on political economy,

including Marx's *Das Kapital*. According to Anna Ulyanova's memoirs, published before the legend of Lenin
had taken firm shape, Vladimir did not even look at—
let alone read—the books belonging to his brother, with
whom he was sharing a room. At that time, she reports,
he showed no interest at all in politics or economics
and did not have any definite political views.[35] He was
engrossed in Turgenev's *Rudin*, *A Nest of Gentlefolk*,
On the Eve, *Fathers and Sons*, and *Smoke*—novels
which he read several times that summer. According to
Lenin's own admission, as we shall see, he did not
really "discover" Chernyshevsky until the summer of
1887, after the execution of his brother, and did not become acquainted with Marx until 1888–89. As Valentinov has aptly put it, the story of Vladimir Ulyanov's
early revolutionism is a fairy tale.[36]

The Execution of Alexander

On March 1, 1887, an event in Saint Petersburg changed
forever the trajectory of Vladimir Ulyanov's life and,
with it, the course of Russian and world history. On
that day—the sixth anniversary of the death of Czar
Alexander II at the hands of revolutionary terrorists—
Sasha Ulyanov was arrested for his participation in a
conspiracy to assassinate Czar Alexander III. Unknown
to his family, Lenin's brother had joined a group of
revolutionary students who, unable to find any other
form of effective and meaningful political activity, turned
to terror and resolved to revive the traditions of *Narodnaia Volia* ("The People's Will" or "The People's Freedom"—the word *"volia"* carries both meanings).

By 1887 terrorism had become an important part of

the Russian revolutionary tradition. In 1866 D. V. Kara-
kozov made the first attempt on the life of the czar—
an act to which the government responded with its own
kind of "white terror." In 1878 Vera Zasulich, the future prominent Russian Marxist with whom Lenin collaborated for a time on *Iskra,* tried unsuccessfully to
assassinate General Trepov, the Saint Petersburg city
governor, for ordering the flogging of a political prisoner.
In the same year, S. M. Kravchinsky, acting with un-
precedented boldness and daring, assassinated the Chief
of Police, General Mezentsov. The year 1879 saw the
assassination of A. Kropotkin, the governor of Kharkov,
by G. D. Goldenberg; Leon Mirsky's attempt on the life
of General Drenteln, Mezentsov's successor; and attempts on the life of the czar by A. Solov'ev, A. Zheliabov, A. Mikhailov, and others. In 1880, in yet another
attempt on the life of the czar, S. Khalturin organized
an explosion in the Winter Palace which killed eleven
people and wounded fifty-six. On March 1, 1881, finally,
the wave of terrorism crested when Alexander II, the
Czar-Liberator who at one time had advocated a revolution from above in order to avoid one from below, was
mortally wounded by a bomb thrown by a member of
Narodnaia Volia when his carriage passed along the
Catherine Canal in Saint Petersburg.

In January of 1887, when Alexander Ulyanov became a member of the Terrorist Section of *Narodnaia
Volia,* he was in the midst of a brilliant career at Saint
Petersburg University; a year before, he had received the
gold medal for a competitive essay and his research in
biology. He was strongly thinking about becoming a
professor. Dreamy, withdrawn even within the circle of
his family, completely absorbed by his study of the
natural world, an extremely sensitive young man who

subjected himself to a strict moral and ethical code, Sasha Ulyanov seemed to be a most unlikely candidate for the role of revolutionary and assassin. What prompted this fateful metamorphosis from scientist to revolutionary?

There is evidence that, like many other students, he found the reactionary atmosphere in the capital and especially at the university stultifying and depressing. In his letters to his family he detailed some of the government's moves against the students: the suppression of all student organizations, the closing of all student canteens, the prevention of all demonstrations. Deeply affected by the death of his father—he is reported to have contemplated suicide when the news reached him —he continued with his program of study. But his mind increasingly turned to socioeconomic and political questions. During his last summer at Kokushkino he spent hours reading the first volume of *Das Kapital*, as well as other socialist literature in French, English, and German. He finally became convinced that refusal to join the revolutionary movement was tantamount to accepting the oppressive autocratic order. When on November 17, 1886, the government used Cossack troops to arrest a crowd of students who had assembled at the Volkovo cemetery to commemorate the twenty-fifth anniversary of the death of N. A. Dobroliubov—known to all educated Russians from the pages of *Sovremennik* and *Svistok* as an indomitable critic of the autocracy— the first member of the Ulyanov family became a revolutionary.

The news of Alexander's arrest and participation in the plot to assassinate the czar struck the Ulyanov family like a bolt of lightning out of the blue sky.[37] Not even Anna, who at that time also studied in Saint Petersburg and was very close to Sasha, knew about his involvement in the revolutionary movement. For Vladimir Ulyanov, the sudden and unexpected discovery of this aspect of his brother's life and personality came as a shattering and consequential revelation. Having frequently ridiculed his brother for his intense interest in the natural sciences, Vladimir now had to admit the existence of a dimension in Sasha's life of which he had been totally unaware. While the requisite data for a full assessment of Vladimir's psychological reaction to his brother's arrest and subsequent execution are unfortunately lacking, the available evidence suggests that he reproached himself severely for his strained relationship with Sasha, for having failed to understand him.[38] During the summer of 1887 he would try diligently to learn all he could about his brother's life in Saint Petersburg from Anna and from I. Chebotarev, who had been Alexander's roommate. Putting his questions "quietly" and "methodically," young Lenin is reported to have been particularly interested in his brother's revolutionary outlook and his conduct at the trial, which Alexander Ulyanov, following the example of Zheliabov, had used to deliver a ringing denunciation of the autocracy.[39]

Discipline was a family trait and virtue among the Ulyanovs. During his final examinations at the Gymnasium, which coincided with the time of his brother's execution, the young Lenin demonstrated an almost unbelievable power of concentration and ability to control his emotions, as well as a deadly efficiency. Even after the news of the execution had reached Simbirsk and had become the greatest scandal in the history of the town, Vladimir Ulyanov—who had already completed a whole battery of examinations on previous days—calmly translated passages from Thucydides into Russian and

solved problems in trigonometry. Completing his examination papers earlier than anyone else and being the first
to leave the examination room, he passed all tests with
flying colors. The performance of his sister Olga, a year
younger, was equally brilliant. She, too, was awarded
the gold medal. The school authorities, however, decided
that it would be inappropriate to engrave the Ulyanov
name in the marble plaque honoring the other recipients
of this distinction.[40]

In spite of his discipline and self-control, there is
no doubt that the world of Vladimir Ulyanov collapsed
under the weight of his brother's fate. D. M. Andreev,
a schoolmate who had a chance encounter with him
shortly after the execution of Sasha, recalls that Vladimir's grief choked off his voice. "I saw Volodia's deep
sorrow and sensed a spirit of firm determination which
somehow filled him especially at that moment. . . ." [41]
According to his sister Anna, he became "grim and
taciturn." V. V. Kashkadamova, a teacher, noticed that
after Sasha's execution there was a sharp change in
Vladimir. "He ceased to joke, rarely smiled, and somehow all of a sudden became an adult. Only in his relations with the younger children did he remain the
former gay and affectionate Volodia. . . ." [42] Thus, underneath the calm exterior of Vladimir Ulyanov there
were concealed an intense emotional involvement and
deep crisis. When, as one biographer of Lenin has put
it, the autocracy reached into his home and extinguished
its brightest light, it also wounded Vladimir Ulyanov
to the core.

In czarist Russia of the 1880s, young men and
women, especially students, never had to search long
for good reasons to rebel against the political and social
reality which surrounded them. It is conceivable that

these reasons alone, in due course, would have induced Vladimir Ulyanov to become a revolutionary. Certainly this period of Russian history produced scores of revolutionaries whose initial direct confrontation with the autocracy did not involve a traumatic experience like the execution of a brother. Revolution was in the air. Educated and sensitive Russians voiced legitimate grievances against the political authority to which they were subject —a regime which did not tolerate open discussion of social issues and elevated even the most moderate attempt to bring about social change to a state crime. Yet the evidence is compelling that it was the shock of the execution and his subsequent attempt to reconstruct and understand the *Gedankenwelt* of his brother, to comprehend Sasha's motivations and concerns, which triggered the transformation of Vladimir Ulyanov into Lenin. When he was arrested for the first time and a fellow student asked him what he intended to do after his release, Lenin replied: "What is there to think? My path has been blazed by my older brother." [43] According to his sister Anna, Sasha's fate "had an exceedingly powerful impact on Vladimir . . . and, taken by itself, provided a strong impetus toward a revolutionary path." [44] In an eight-line "Unfinished Autobiography," written in April of 1917 in response to a letter to the Petrograd Soviet from a committee of soldiers inquiring about the Bolshevik leader, Lenin wrote: "My name is Vladimir Ilyich Ulyanov. I was born in Simbirsk on April 10, 1870. In the spring of 1887, my older brother, Alexander, was executed by Alexander III for an attempt (March 1, 1887) on his life. . . ." [45] If Lenin rarely spoke about his brother Alexander and never mentioned him in his letters to his family,[46] this fact cannot be ascribed to a lack of emotion. On the contrary, the memory of Sasha was too painful to be recalled. In spite of their childhood rivalries and disagreements, he had loved his brother deeply. During much of his life Alexander had been his model and hero. There is no doubt that the memory of his martyred brother was forever burned into Lenin's soul.

Measured by the political practices of Soviet Russia, whose contours were to be so decisively shaped by Lenin only thirty years later, the czarist government showed remarkable leniency, tolerance, and even magnanimity in its treatment of the Ulyanov family. The considerable state pension which Lenin's mother was granted after the death of her husband was continued and, at least initially, none of the Ulyanov children—with the exception of Anna, who had been studying in Saint Petersburg at the time of the assassination attempt—were barred from the pursuit of a higher education because of Alexander's terrorist activities. In response to a petition by her mother and in recognition of its inability to prove her involvement in the March 1 affair, the government revoked Anna's original sentence of five years' exile in Siberia; instead, she was allowed to live with her family in Kokushkino—albeit under open police surveillance. Like any other family, the Ulyanovs were permitted to own, inherit, buy and sell property. Their freedom of movement was not unduly restricted. In September 1888, for example, the entire Ulyanov family, including Anna and Vladimir—who, as we shall see, had by this time also been exiled to Kokushkino for participating in a student demonstration—was allowed to move to Kazan. As a matter of fact, even after Lenin's first direct clash with the police authorities, his expulsion from the university, and his exile, the czarist government allowed him to prepare himself outside the regular channels for a professional career. Thus, ironical as it may seem, the biography of the Ulyanov family, and especially of the young Lenin, furnishes interesting material for a case study of the differences between nineteenth-century authoritarian government and twentieth-century totalitarianism.

On the Road to Revolution

Truth is one of the first casualties of any totalitarian regime, regardless of its specific ideological complexion —whether it be the notorious "technique of the big lie" associated with the regime of a Hitler or Goebbels, the "power of the glittering phrase" of which Boris Pasternak speaks so eloquently in *Dr. Zhivago*, or the more subtle and frequently less easily discernible falsification of history, the distortion of the past, so frequently employed by dictators in their attempt to justify the present.

The distortion of Lenin's life, personality, and intellectual development began in some ways during his lifetime. After his death, however, it quickly assumed the monstrous proportions of a cult which Lenin himself would never have tolerated—a cult which all but destroyed the human figure of Lenin, replacing it with the caricature of a superman and idealized hero-in-the-abstract. Increasingly, the features of this synthetic Lenin were projected backward in time, and Lenin's life and personality development were portrayed as a kind of Nevskii Prospekt, i.e., a straight and wide thoroughfare, leading from childhood to revolution. The requirements of this cult, especially during the time of its eclipse by that of Stalin, dictated the publication of certain kinds of information about Lenin and the suppression or with-holding of other facts. Much documentary material re-lating to the 1880s and 1890s, for example, including the memoirs of his brother Dimitri, has remained un-published.[1] As a result, the biographer faces enormous difficulties in his attempt to reconstruct the crucial period from 1887 to 1900 during which Lenin became a revolutionary and ultimately the author of the peculiar political doctrine known to the world as Bolshevism.

In a speech before the plenary session of the Mos-cow Soviet, convened in memory of Lenin on February 7, 1924—scarcely a fortnight after his death—Maria Ilyi-nichna, the youngest of the Ulyanov children, provided the "factual" basis for the widespread Soviet fiction that, already as a seventeen-year-old, Lenin had developed the basic principles of his revolutionary program and Marx-ist *Weltanschauung*. She ascribed to Lenin the following words, supposedly uttered when he learned of his broth-er's execution: "No, we shall not take that road [i.e., the road of terror]. We must take a different road." [2] In Soviet historiography this statement has been interpreted to mean that as early as 1887 Lenin had come to regard terrorism as an inappropriate approach to revolution and was looking for a "different path," namely, Marxism.

Aside from the fact that Maria Ulyanova was only nine years old in 1887, we have the testimony of her sister Anna that Lenin "did not have any definite po-litical views at that time," as well as Lenin's own state-ment that he did not read *Das Kapital* until the begin-ning of 1889.[3] Moreover, a careful examination of the available evidence suggests that Lenin began his career as a revolutionary precisely by taking the road which his brother had chosen: his first contacts with the revolutionary movement involved adherents of the terrorist traditions of *Narodnaia Volia*. This finding is not only consistent with our attempt to interpret the psychology of the young Lenin at the time of his brother's execution, but also tends to confirm the view that it was the search to understand the world of Alexander which induced Lenin to abandon Turgenev in favor of Chernyshevsky and Marx, and to exchange what promised to be a brilliant academic or professional career for the uncertain and precarious fate of a revolutionary. Much more credible than the testimony of Maria Ulyanova are the recollections of V. V. Kashkadamova, a close friend of the Ulyanov family, who reports that Lenin, after learning of Alexander's participation in the conspiracy and his arrest, frequently repeated: "This means, he had to act this way; he could not act otherwise." [4]

Lenin spent the summer following his graduation from the Simbirsk Gymnasium on the family estate in Kokushkino. Relieved from the pressures of schoolwork and final examinations, he now had to come to grips with the memory of Alexander, his own changed role in the family, and the terrible grief of his mother, "whom one must now help with various everyday matters." In spite of the fortitude and moral courage which Maria Aleksandrovna displayed in the presence of her family, her solicitude and concern for her other children, her attempt to shield and protect them as much as possible from the consequences of what had happened, there is little doubt that Lenin and his brother and sisters felt the impact of Alexander's fate. The sudden change in the outward appearance of their mother alone must have brought home to the Ulyanov children the full depth of her suffering and agony. Maria Aleksandrovna, who had gone to Saint Petersburg to attend the trial of her son, is reported to have turned gray overnight after Sasha's execution. There is some evidence that this tragic event, coming less than a year and a half after the death of her husband, brought this remarkable woman to the brink of insanity.[5]

The tragedy of Sasha's execution and the resulting ostracism by the community—which Lenin would remember throughout his life—drew the Ulyanovs even closer together, especially on Kokushkino, where every corner reminded them of Alexander and where the numbing sadness of the present was constantly disturbed by the pleasant memories of the past, as well as by the sympathetic and compassionate, yet jarring, questions of the relatives who came there for the summer. They all knew that Sasha had "especially loved" Kokushkino, whose surroundings had been his first "scientific laboratory," giving him scope for his early awakened interest in the natural sciences. It was on the estate in Kokushkino during the previous summer that they had been together as a family for the last time.

For the young Lenin, the summer of 1887 must have been especially difficult. As a seventeen-year-old he now suddenly became the head of a large household. Together with Anna, he made every effort to help his mother and his younger brother and sisters. Piecing together fragments of information from a variety of sources, one is drawn to the conclusion that Vladimir Ulyanov grew up and matured beyond his years during that summer. When N. Veretennikov, a cousin who had known Lenin from childhood, saw him at Kokushkino in July 1887, he noticed a sharp change in his former playmate. Volodia had become reserved, smiled rarely, and was sparing of words. Although he had not changed in appearance, he had suddenly turned into "a grown-up, serious individual." [6]

In the fall of 1887 Lenin enrolled in the Faculty of Law at Kazan University. Following the advice of F. M. Kerensky, the director of the Simbirsk Gymnasium, and her own inclinations not to let Vladimir go off to the university by himself, Maria Aleksandrovna had chosen her husband's alma mater, one of the provincial universities,[7] and moved her family to the city of Kazan. Lenin's decision to study jurisprudence instead of philology came as a surprise and disappointment to his former teachers, who regarded history and foreign languages as the forte of their star pupil, and to G. N. Shebuev, a lecturer in mathematical physics at Kazan University, who visited the Ulyanovs in the summer of 1887 and, in the course of long conversations with Vladimir, became convinced that young Lenin, like his father, had a definitely "mathematical bent of mind." When questioned by his cousin as to why he decided to study jurisprudence, Lenin supposedly replied that at a different time he might have chosen to pursue other sciences, but that now was the time to study the science of law and political economy.

Lenin's university career, however, which began with courses on theology (a required subject in all faculties), the history of Russian law, the history of Roman law, and English, was short-lived. On September 2, 1887, he signed a pledge, required of all students, not to become a member of any associations, including legally recognized societies, or to take part in any organizations, without prior permission from the authorities. Two days later he joined a student circle which, in the judgment of the police, was revolutionary and manifested "an exceedingly harmful orientation." He also became a member of an association of students from Samara and Simbirsk which sponsored an illegal student cafeteria. Sometime prior to December 1, the members of this group elected Lenin as their representative to the all-university council of associations. In this capacity Vladimir Ulyanov attended a secret meeting at the university on December 1, 1887, with students from Moscow University to learn about the demonstrations that had taken place in the old capital at the end of November to protest the reactionary university statute of 1884 and a circular from the Minister of Public Education, dated June 18, 1887, which effectively barred the children of the lower classes from access to secondary and higher education.[8]

When the student inspector appeared at this meeting and asked the students to disperse, he was roughed up, just as his opposite number in Moscow had been earlier. A plea to the students by a group of professors was equally ineffectual. Emboldened by their "success," the students now passed a number of resolutions and drew up a petition to the rector of the university. While the petition was primarily concerned with student and university affairs, it definitely carried wider political overtones. In the preamble to the petition, for example, the students spoke of the "impossible conditions of Russian life in general and student life in particular," as well as their "desire to call the attention of society to these conditions. . . ." In addition to the usual and traditional demands for their own libraries, reading rooms, cafeterias, and mutual aid funds, they demanded identical regulations and statutes for all Russian universities; government of the university by a board of professors without any outside interference; the establishment of a public student court, "whose decisions the board of professors cannot ignore"; the right of the students to award all scholarships and fellowships through their elected representatives; and the readmission of all students who had been expelled from Russian universities for participating in various kinds of disturbances. Finally, claiming to speak for themselves as well as for all of Russian society, the students expressed their indignation at the officials responsible for the brutal violence committed against their fellow students in Moscow and demanded the punishment of those officials.

The reaction of the authorities was both predictable and swift. Lectures and other activities at the university were suspended for two months. Over a hundred students—more than one-eighth of the entire student body—were arrested, among them Vladimir Ulyanov. It was now that his kinship to Alexander became a factor which directly influenced his treatment by the authorities. Although there was no evidence that Lenin had played a major role in the demonstration, he was among the first group of thirty-nine students to be expelled outright. Within a short time, more than a hundred students were either excluded from the university or asked to resign.[9] Lenin, too, withdrew from the university in a further gesture of defiance, declaring in a petition to the rector that he found it "impossible to continue my education at the university given the existing conditions of university life." [10]

Thus, within less than seven months after Alexander's execution, young Lenin had experienced his first open collision with the authorities, had spent two days in prison, and had drawn his first exile sentence. Like most Russian revolutionaries in the nineteenth century, he had received his baptism of fire as a participant in a student demonstration. Without realizing it at the time, he had taken the first consequential and fatal step toward becoming a lifelong revolutionary.

In Search of Alexander

Following Sasha's example, Lenin had kept his involvement in the student movement a strict secret. His arrest and subsequent expulsion from the university, therefore, came as a complete surprise to his family. Lenin himself, however, must have been fully aware of the likely consequences of his activities. Whether he attracted the attention of revolutionary student circles because he was the brother of Alexander Ulyanov, who by then was revered as a hero and martyr by many students, or whether he himself actively sought involvement in the revolutionary movement, is not definitely known. The available evidence suggests that within a few weeks after his arrival in Kazan young Lenin came into contact with, and soon afterward joined, one of the most radical organizations then in existence in the city. Moreover, he seems to have deliberately cultivated relationships with older students. He was the youngest of the thirty-nine students who were immediately expelled from the university; by far the majority of the active participants in the demonstration belonged to the generation of his brother Alexander.

Both the speed and the depth of Lenin's involvement in revolutionary circles at the university were unusual for a first-semester student. If Vladimir Ulyanov, who had established an impeccable record of good conduct and the reputation of a model student in the Gymnasium, aware of his mother's fears and fully cognizant of the potential consequences of his activities for himself and for his family, nevertheless chose to take part in revolutionary student circles and illegal associations, he must have had compelling reasons. What were they?

Unfortunately, the future Bolshevik leader left us virtually no autobiographical information, and there is no empirical evidence which could throw light on this crucial stage in his life. However, it stands to reason that the involvement of Vladimir Ulyanov in the student movement and in revolutionary circles in Kazan represented the first phase of his attempt to penetrate and to understand that aspect of Alexander's life and spiritual world which had remained a closed book for him. Psychologically speaking, his involvement in the revolutionary movement, at least initially, was the result of his desire to expiate his guilt for having failed to understand Sasha and for having frequently ridiculed him through identifying himself with the cause for which Alexander had made the supreme sacrifice.

Significantly, the first revolutionary group which Lenin joined in Kazan was the circle headed by Lazar Bogoraz, whose avowed purpose it was to revive *Narodnaia Volia* and to accomplish successfully the task which Alexander Ulyanov and his fellow conspirators had attempted on March 1, 1887. As the police found out a year later, Bogoraz had even succeeded in establishing contact with terrorists in Saint Petersburg.[11] That Lenin himself at this time did, indeed, subscribe to the views of *Narodnaia Volia* is suggested by an episode he related to V. V. Adoratskii in 1905. At the time of his first arrest in Kazan, he told Adoratskii, who had attended the same Faculty of Jurisprudence in which Lenin was enrolled for such a short time, a police officer had asked him: "Why are you rebelling, young man? You are up against a wall!" Lenin's reply—"A wall, yes, but *a rotten one.* Give it a push, and it will come tumbling down!" [12]—reflected the belief of the terrorists that the collapse of the autocracy was imminent and that it would be relatively easy for the revolutionaries to seize political power.

An investigation of Lenin's activities following his expulsion from the university and exile to Kokushkino provides additional evidence of his efforts to understand the revolutionary dimension in Alexander's life. To begin with, there was a remarkable change in his reading habits —a change which before long would lead him to discover the real meaning of Chernyshevsky, to read and understand the works of this progressive writer as Sasha had read and understood them. While Lenin did not totally abandon belles-lettres—he was captivated by Nekrasov at this time and liked Pushkin—he turned increasingly to social criticism. For the first time in his life he became seriously interested in social questions. As it turned out, it was an interest he never abandoned as long as he lived. Moreover, it increasingly crowded out everything else in his life and eventually became all-consuming.

In the years ahead, during which his life gravitated more and more toward the single pursuit of revolution making, Lenin would increasingly deny himself the pleasure of his "addictions"—his love of literature, music, the arts, and chess. As a result, his tastes in literature and art remained relatively undeveloped. Eventually, the merits of all things came to be judged by their relevance to the revolutionary cause. Along with his other passions, this was true of music. Lenin was very fond of Beethoven's *Sonate pathétique*—which may be part of the reason why he was so attracted to Inessa Armand, who reportedly played Beethoven well. Gorky tells us that

Lenin, having listened in rapture to the *Appassionata*, exclaimed that he could listen to it every day. He described it as "marvelous, superhuman music" and expressed his astonishment at the fact that human beings could create such beauty while living in this "vile hell." But listening to music, Lenin confessed to both Lunarcharsky and Gorky, affected his nerves and stirred him up, making him go soft inside, wanting to stroke and pat the heads of the people capable of creating such miracles. This he could not afford to let happen because "you might get your hand bitten off." In any case, "one has to beat their heads without mercy—although ideally we are against any sort of force." Thus Lenin developed the asceticism and tendency toward self-castigation which Peter Struve, a collaborator of Lenin in the 1890s, noticed and remarked about. And as a result of his single-mindedness of purpose and personal asceticism, Lenin would leave to the Russian people the unfortunate legacy of a strictly utilitarian approach to the arts, which must always poison them in the end.

During the winter of 1887–88, which Lenin, together with his family, spent in the in some ways desirable isolation of Kokushkino, he assiduously worked his way through the famous "thick journals" that he found in his father's library and among the books left by an uncle. He now acquainted himself with the works of the progressive writers of the 1860s and 1870s, notably N. G. Chernyshevsky, the famous editor of *Sovremennik (The Contemporary)*, who had been the leading radical publicist of his time. As Lenin was to recall in 1904, "never in my later life, not even when I was in prison in St. Petersburg and in exile in Siberia, did I read so much as during the year of my exile from Kazan." [13] He read and reread—in the same issues his brother had held in his hands—Chernyshevsky's ponderous essays in *Sovremennik*, as well as his utopian novel *What Is to Be Done?*—the book which had become the "bible" for a generation of Russian revolutionaries and which had been one of Alexander's favorite works. Whereas the novel had made no impression on Lenin when he read it for the first time at the age of fourteen, it had an extraordinary and incredible impact on him when he reread it three years later—this time already with pencil in hand, taking copious notes and writing summaries in notebooks which he "kept for a long time."

These notebooks, unfortunately, seem to have been lost; however, we have Lenin's own testimony that the message of the "archbishop of propaganda," as Herzen once aptly characterized Chernyshevsky, "ploughed me over . . . completely." When in 1904 Nikolai Valentinov, then a fellow Bolshevik and revolutionary comrade-in-arms, called into question the literary merits of *What Is to Be Done?*, Lenin turned on him like a tiger. Without any qualms whatsoever, he argued from the revolutionary impact of a work of literature to its talented and sophisticated style and literary merit—a good example of his peculiar logic and a portent of things to come. Defending the novel of Chernyshevsky, whose language he placed on a level with that of Turgenev and Tolstoy,[14] Lenin made the following illuminating statement:

I declare that it is inadmissible to call *What Is To Be Done?* primitive and untalented. Under its influence hundreds of people became revolutionaries. Could this be if Chernyshevsky wrote in an untalented and primitive style? Chernyshevsky's novel, for example, fascinated and captivated my brother. It also captivated me. *It ploughed me over again completely.* When did you read *What Is To Be Done?* It is useless to read it when your mother's milk has not yet dried on your lips. Chernyshevsky's novel is too complex, too full of thoughts and ideas, in order to be understood and valued at a young age. I myself tried to read it . . . when I was fourteen years old . . . it was a worthless and superficial reading that did not lead to anything. But then, *after the execution of my brother, knowing that Chernyshevsky's novel was one of his most favorite works, I began what was a real reading and pored over the book, not several days, but several weeks.* Only then did I understand its full depth. It is a work which gives one a charge for a whole life. Untalented works cannot have such influence.[15]

In her memoirs, Krupskaya, Lenin's wife, drew attention to the tremendous impact which Chernyshevsky had on Lenin and recalled her surprise at learning how attentively her husband had read *What Is to Be Done?* During his exile in Siberia, Lenin kept an album containing photographs of the writers who had exerted the greatest influence on him: in addition to pictures of Marx, Engels, Herzen and Pisarev, there were two photographs of Chernyshevsky. In 1908 he reread Chernyshevsky and in his work *Materialism and Emperiocriticism,* published in 1909, praised him as a critic of Kant and "as the only really great Russian writer who—from the Fifties until 1888—was able to maintain a position based on an integral philosophical materialism and to reject the pitiful nonsense of the neo-Kantians, positivists, Machists, and other muddleheads." [16] Even after the Revolution, when Lenin was constantly confronted with pressing political problems, he always had a complete set of Chernyshevsky's writings in his Kremlin office—along with those of Marx, Engels, and Plekhanov. If we can rely on the testimony of Krupskaya, it was to the works of Chernyshevsky that Lenin turned in his free moments.

Thus, more than a year before Lenin encountered Marx, he fell under the spell of Chernyshevsky. It was Chernyshevsky, not Hegel or Marx, who introduced Lenin to dialectical materialism; it was Chernyshevsky who infected Lenin with a lifelong hatred of liberalism in all its forms, a hatred which became submerged from time to time but was never fully extinguished; it was Chernyshevsky, finally, who instilled in Lenin a profound disregard for the problem of means and ends in politics.[17] When in the winter of 1888–89 Lenin began reading *Das Kapital,* his understanding and interpretation of Marx already reflected perspectives which he had derived from Chernyshevsky. What was it in Chernyshevsky that captivated the imagination of the seventeen-year-old Vladimir Ulyanov and helped to transform him into Lenin, the greatest revolutionary of all time?

The Birth of V. I. Lenin

According to Lenin's own testimony, he was impressed by Chernyshevsky's "depth of thought," by the "encyclopedic nature of [his] knowledge," by the "clarity of his revolutionary views, and his merciless polemical talent." In Lenin's view, Chernyshevsky was one of the few men who, like Marx, possessed "an absolute and perfect revolutionary feeling." His greatest contribution, according to Lenin, lay in the fact that "he not only demonstrated the necessity of every correctly thinking and really honest man to become a revolutionary, but also . . . *what the revolutionary must be like, what his rules must be, how he must go about attaining his goals, and by what methods and means he can bring about their realization.*" As Lenin told V. V. Vorovskii in 1904, it was the novel

What Is to Be Done?, with its utopian vision of a socialist society patterned after Fourier, Owen, and Louis Blanc, which "exerted the main overwhelming revolutionary influence on me . . . before my acquaintance with the works of Marx, Engels, and Plekhanov." [18]

Like scores of other Russian revolutionaries in the second half of the nineteenth century, Lenin was inspired by Chernyshevsky's hero Rakhmetov, the revolutionary who denies himself the pleasures of life, sleeps on a bed of nails, and leads an ascetic existence, pursuing with singular determination and fanatic dedication his sole purpose in life: to prepare and steel himself for the coming social revolution. Rakhmetov was Chernyshevsky's answer to Lermontov's Pechorin, Pushkin's Onegin, Goncharov's Oblomov, and Turgenev's Rudin —the "superfluous men" of Russian literature, in themselves expressions and reflections of the malaise of Russian society under the czars. *What Is to Be Done?* was an apotheosis of the "new men and women," the "flower of the best people," the "salt of the salt of the earth"— in short, the revolutionaries who would transform the world. In thinly veiled language, the novel proclaimed social and political liberation, complete equality, and the emancipation of women—all to be accomplished by the "strong personalities" who would impose their character on the direction of events.

Given the requisite psychological inclinations, Chernyshevsky's novel could be read as a celebration of the potential power of a determined individual, as a glorification of the human will. Although *What Is to Be Done?* goes to great lengths in proclaiming the natural goodness of man and overtly extols the virtues of equality and democracy, it is really an open panegyric to elitism, a eulogy to the vanguard which moves history, a celebration of violence committed by the new men in the interest of equality, justice, and progress. The novel, moreover, reflects the author's incredible condescension, if not contempt, toward the masses, as well as his intellectual arrogance and downright snobbery. Thus, for example, Maria Aleksevna, the mother of the novel's heroine, is derided for not knowing more than five words of French. Kirsanov, one of the "new men," felt nothing more than pity for Nastenka, his virtuous prostitute, who "was never a match for him, for they were not equals in intellectual development." And although Chernyshevsky denounced the Russian aristocracy, he described at length the distinguished genealogy of Rakhmetov, his revolutionary hero.

This, then, was the political tract which inspired hundreds of Russian revolutionaries, among them young Lenin, who during the summer of 1888 alone read it no less than five times.[19] Writing in 1894, G. V. Plekhanov, the "father of Russian Marxism" and future teacher of Lenin, was to characterize Chernyshevsky's novel as the greatest success in the history of Russian publishing, as a work from which "we all have drawn moral strength and faith in a better future." [20] And when Lenin in 1902 laid down the principles of Bolshevism in what was probably his single most important political pamphlet, he paid tribute to his former mentor by giving it the title *What Is to Be Done?*

In the fall of 1888, the Ulyanovs moved back to Kazan. Lenin's repeated attempts to gain readmission to the university met with failure. For a period of three and a half years, he faced an uncertain future, condemned to lead the kind of existence which would have spelled doom for a man who did not have his iron discipline, determination, and willpower. While there is some evidence that Lenin occasionally suffered from moodiness, irritability, and feelings of depression during this time—in one of her petitions to the government his mother expressed fear that he might commit suicide [21] —generally speaking he seems to have made constructive use of his idle time. Drawing up a detailed work schedule for himself, he studied from morning till night, acquiring his own kind of university education.

It was not until May 1891 that the authorities granted him permission to take the examinations in jurisprudence as an external student at Saint Petersburg University—examinations he passed with flying colors a few days before his sister Olga, then a student in the capital, died of typhus. In November 1891 Lenin obtained his law degree *magna cum laude* and soon after was admitted to the bar. He began his practice of law with the firm of A. N. Khardin, a liberal, in Samara, and in the fall of 1893 became associated with the firm of M. F. Volkenstein, also a liberal, in Saint Petersburg.[22]

In the years between 1888 and the beginning of his short-lived career as a lawyer, however, he had not only read university textbooks and prepared himself assiduously for the law examinations, but he had also tried his hand at farming a small estate his mother had purchased for 7,500 rubles near the village of Alakaevka in the vicinity of Samara—a venture which Lenin soon gave up because, as he told Krupskaya later on, his "relations with the peasants became abnormal." He had become acquainted with Marx and Plekhanov, as well as with a number of writings by N. E. Fedoseev, a brilliant young Russian Marxist whose ideas he came to value very highly.[23] Finally, with law examinations on his mind, he had utilized his stay in Saint Petersburg to make further inquiries about his brother Alexander.[24]

While preparing himself for a career in law, Lenin had also—consciously or unconsciously—laid the foundation for what was to become his real profession.

Most important for our study is the fact that for six years, from 1887 to 1893, during his formative period as a revolutionary, Lenin was in close contact with revolutionaries who believed in the terrorist tradition of *Narodnaia Volia*. His involvement in the Bogoraz circle has already been mentioned. During his second stay in Kazan, Lenin became acquainted with Maria Chetvergova, a well-known follower of *Narodnaia Volia*, and joined her circle. This group belonged to a nationwide organization established by M. V. Sabunaev for the express purpose of reviving *Narodnaia Volia*.[25] Chetvergova was not only an admirer of the heroic struggle of the terrorists, but she also worshiped Chernyshevsky. Lenin told Krupskaya later on that he did not know anyone "with whom one could talk as pleasantly and profitably about Chernyshevsky as with Chetvergova."[26] Twelve years later, on his return from exile in Siberia, he stopped and paid a visit to her in Ufa.

Growing increasingly apprehensive about Vladimir's involvement with revolutionaries in Kazan, Maria Aleksandrovna moved her family to Samara (now Kuibyshev). But here, too, young Lenin soon established contacts with Jacobin radicals and followers of *Narodnaia Volia*. In 1889 Samara was full of political prisoners and exiles—participants in the famous "movement to the people" of the early 1870s and adherents of the later terrorist movements. Before long Lenin was in contact with N. S. Dolgov,[27] who at one time had been a follower of S. G. Nechaev, the Russian Jacobin par excellence and the *enfant terrible* of the Russian revolutionary movement, who inspired the character of Petr

Verkhovensky in Dostoevsky's *Besy* (*The Demons*, also translated as *The Possessed*). Through Dolgov Lenin became acquainted with M. P. Golubeva-Iasneva and A. I. Romanova, both members of the Jacobin group organized by P. G. Zaichnevskii. In her memoirs, Golubeva, whose brother had been Lenin's English professor at Kazan University, relates that her Jacobin orientation immediately aroused young Lenin's attention, and that at this time he was greatly interested in the question of the "seizure of power" and questioned neither its feasibility nor its desirability.[28] Finally, in Samara Lenin also joined the circle of A. P. Skliarenko, a Populist group whose members were followers of *Narodnaia Volia* before their conversion to Marxism later on.[29]

Some Soviet historians would have us believe that already during his stay in Kazan Lenin was a Marxist and a member of Marxist circles—those of N. E. Fedoseev or M. L. Mandel'shtam.[30] However, the usual elaborate archive documentation which one has come to expect from Soviet research on Lenin is missing in this case. Moreover, Lenin himself made it clear in 1922 that, although he had heard of Fedoseev and corresponded with him, he had never personally met him,[31] and nowhere in his writings did Lenin refer to being a member in Mandel'shtam's circle.[32]

The available evidence suggests that Lenin did not become seriously interested in Marxism until 1892, when —in the words of his sister Anna—he became preoccupied with the question of "the feasibility of Social Democracy in Russia." [33] As a matter of fact, he spent the first six years of his revolutionary apprenticeship in close contact with some of the most outstanding Jacobin radicals in the Russian revolutionary movement and with adherents of the terrorist orientation of *Narodnaia*

Volia. Years later, Lenin wrote in *What Is to Be Done?* that "many [of the Social Democrats] began to develop a revolutionary frame of mind as *narodovol'tsy* [i.e., followers of *Narodnaia Volia*]. In their early youth almost all of them bowed in exaltation before the heroes of terror. Rejecting the fascinating impression of this heroic tradition required a struggle [and] was accompanied by a break with the people who at all costs wanted to remain true to *Narodnaia Volia* and for whom the young Social Democrats had high respect." [34] When Krupskaya cited this passage in her memoirs, she added that this paragraph represented a piece of Lenin's autobiography.

Throughout his life, Lenin preserved his admiration for the heroic deeds of *Narodnaia Volia* and, as his sister Anna tells us, "always felt a deep regard for the old *narodovol'tsy*." [35] When in 1902 S. V. Balmashov, a nineteen-year-old Social Revolutionary—the Social Revolutionaries or SRs were the heirs of *Narodnaia Volia*—assassinated D. S. Sipiagin, the czarist Interior Minister, Lenin, then living in London, exclaimed: "A neat job!" [36] Indeed, Lenin never completely freed himself from his Jacobin past; the vestiges of *Narodnaia Volia* which I. Lalaiants noticed in 1893 remained with him to the end.

For an assessment of Lenin it is both interesting and significant that he never openly revealed his involvement with Jacobin and terrorist groups in the 1880s and 1890s. When he filled out a party questionnaire in 1921 and replied to the question of when and where his participation in the revolutionary movement had begun, he answered: "In 1892–1893, in Samara." [37] Did Lenin's career as a revolutionary not begin, in his thinking, until 1892–93, when he became a Marxist? This is difficult to believe! It is more likely that Lenin wanted to con-

ceal his Jacobin past, especially since his political opponents had often charged him with being a Jacobin
and pursuing a Blanquist revolutionary strategy.[38] While
it can be argued that by 1921 his concept of meaningful
revolutionary activity recognized only the Bolshevik version of Marxism and precluded all other orientations
in the revolutionary movement, there is no doubt that
Lenin was fully aware of his beginnings as a revolutionary. Whatever his reasons were, in concealing the
true nature of his initial involvement in the revolutionary
movement Lenin resorted to the distortion of the truth
which was to become so characteristic of the cult created
around his life and personality after his death in 1924
—the distortion of the truth which resulted in the repeated rape of history under Stalin and, in a larger sense,
developed into one of the salient features of the Soviet
political regime.

THE SEARCH
FOR A THEORY OF REVOLUTION

卍 卍 卍

The political ideas which Lenin developed in the course
of his thirteen-year-long quest for a solution to the problem of revolution in Russia must be regarded as among
the most important contributions to political theory in
the twentieth century. In one of his perceptive essays,
Bertram Wolfe has called Lenin "the architect of twentieth-century totalitarianism" and has described him as
"a man who changed the world into which he was born
beyond all recognition." [1] Assessing the influence of the
Bolshevik leader fifty years after the Russian Revolution, Leonard Schapiro has spoken of him as the "strange
and troubled genius, whose personal impact on events
both in his own country and in the world outside may
well have been greater than that of any other individual
in this century." [2] Lenin's place in the annals of world
history is assured because he became the prophet of a
new dogmatic and intolerant religious faith, namely,
militant communism, a political creed which centered
around the wholesale repudiation of the Western way of
life and the condemnation of all existing political institutions, a creed which openly proclaimed the legitimacy
of dictatorship and inspired a novel political institution,
by now a hallmark of our century: the one-party state.
Perhaps no one has better expressed the significance of
Lenin for our age than did Boris Pasternak in his novel
Dr. Zhivago:

... the whole of [the] nineteenth century—its revolutions in Paris, its generations of Russian exiles starting with Herzen, its assassinations of Tsars . . . the whole of the worker's movement of the world, the whole of Marxism in the parliaments and universities of Europe, the whole of this new system of ideas with its newness, the swiftness of its conclusion, its irony, and its pitiless remedies elaborated in the name of pity—all this was absorbed and expressed in Lenin, who fell upon the old world as the personified retribution for its misdeeds.

And side by side with him there arose before the eyes of the world the vast figure of Russia bursting into flames like a light of redemption for all the sorrows and misfortunes of mankind.[3]

There is little doubt that the course of modern history would have been very different without Lenin. It was Lenin who in 1902, in *What Is to Be Done?*, recognized the Russian peasantry as a potentially revolutionary force and built his theory of revolution around the concept of an alliance between the proletariat and the peasantry—thus, following in the footsteps of Plekhanov, in effect making Marxism applicable to an economically backward and underdeveloped country. It was Lenin who stubbornly defended the notion that without a vanguard the masses would not, and could not, develop revolutionary consciousness—thus divorcing the element of spontaneity (and with it, democracy!) from his revolutionary program. It was Lenin who, against all opposition, insisted on the importance of a small, closely knit, highly centralized, conspiratorial and quasi-military organization of professional revolutionaries, a "fighting organization" composed of men totally dedicated to the destruction of the old and the establishment of a new social order—thus laying the foundation not only for his

political victory in 1917, but also for the party-domi-
nated, future-oriented state society which came into
being in Russia after the October Revolution. It was
Lenin, in short, who fused the Russian revolutionary
tradition of the nineteenth century—especially its voluntarism and its growing preoccupation with organization—
with Marxism into the explosive mixture which in 1917
set Russia "bursting into flames," as Pasternak put it.
Without Lenin, the October Revolution might never
have taken place. And had there been a second Russian
revolution in 1917, it would have been a fundamentally
different one.[4]

The Russian Heritage

Bolshevism, the peculiar blend of revolutionary theory
and action created by Lenin, which was destined to fundamentally alter the face, if not the soul, of Russian
social, economic, and political life, and, in so doing, to
transform the very essence and the realities of international politics on a global scale, is best understood
as an amalgamation of the economic and historical materialism of the Marxist doctrine and the voluntarism
of the Russian revolutionary tradition, as expressed in
Lenin's personality. In Lenin the Marxist we can recognize the *narodovolets* Zheliabov. "History moves too
slowly," Zheliabov had said; "it needs a push." Lenin,
too, believed that history moved too slowly, that it
needed a push. And this push, he thought, could be
provided by a dedicated elite of full-time, professional
revolutionaries, a militant political party—not a party
in the ordinary sense of the word, but one specifically
designed to conduct warfare against the autocracy, a party

organized on the basis of conspiratorial principles as a match for the *okhrana*, the czarist secret police. "Give us an organization of revolutionaries," Lenin was to write in 1902 in *What Is to Be Done?*, "and we shall overturn the whole of Russia."

In the official Communist view, "Leninism is Marxism of the era of imperialism and of the proletarian revolution," to use Stalin's classical formulation. In placing primary emphasis on Lenin's Marxism, Soviet ideologues and historians, with the exception of some writers in the 1920s and early 1930s, have generally tended to minimize his debt to the Russian revolutionary tradition, in spite of the obvious fact that Lenin, as one Western scholar has put it, "was the heir to a movement that had been going on for three quarters of a century." [5] In Soviet historiography today, Lenin's intellectual and political evolution is cautiously linked to the ideas of the "revolutionary democrats," i.e., Herzen, Pisarev, Chernyshevsky, and Dobroliubov; but the prevailing interpretation holds that Lenin's political ideas were mainly inspired by Marx. By contrast, many Western writers, while acknowledging the influence of Marxism, have sought the antecedents of Lenin's political *Weltanschauung* more or less exclusively in one or another orientation of the Russian revolutionary movement of the nineteenth century.

In assessing the relative importance of the two primary formative influences on Lenin, the Russian revolutionary tradition and Marxism, I find that the overwhelming evidence now available points to the former as by far the more significant. Not only did his involvement in the Russian revolutionary movement precede his encounter with Marxism, but it also shaped his whole attitude toward Western Social Democracy. Moreover, while the formative period of his revolutionary development clearly stood under the influence of Chernyshevsky and the Jacobin ideas of *Narodnaia Volia*, Lenin came to be deeply steeped in the *entire* Russian revolutionary tradition; he must be interpreted, therefore, against the background of that tradition and, in a more general and broader sense, against the background of the nineteenth century in Europe, which found a strong reflection in the physiognomy of the Russian revolutionary movement.[6]

By 1887, when Lenin embarked on the road to revolution, the Russian revolutionary or *social* movement (*obshchestvennoe dvizhenie*), as the Russians also call it, had produced an extremely rich and varied tradition. As a matter of fact, there are few ideas in Lenin's political program which he could not have derived from that tradition. Certainly, most of the central concepts of Bolshevism form part of the heritage of the "century of inward revolution" in Russia, to use Berdyaev's term.

Thus, for example, P. I. Pestel (1793–1826), an ardent Russian nationalist of German ancestry, a Lutheran by religion who was willing to use the Orthodox Church to fan the flames of nationalism, had developed the vision of a unitary and uniform Russia, had rejected out of hand the possibility of reform within the existing system, had conceived of democracy as a powerful central government elected but not controlled by the people, and had advocated the elimination of all class distinctions so that social advancement would be exclusively based on service to the state.

Pestel was a leading figure in the famous Decembrist Revolt—an abortive attempt at a *coup d'état* staged for the purpose of constitutional reform on December 14, 1825, by members of the nobility, especially elite guard officers, who were eager to exploit the ignorance and sense of duty of the soldiers of several regiments stationed in Saint Petersburg, as well as to take advantage of the confusion surrounding the succession to the throne by Nicholas I. Although committed to the abolition of serfdom and the eradication of class differences based on birth, Pestel, the most important political theorist among the Decembrists, displayed a strong dictatorial temperament, as well as the taste for violence and coercion in the name of noble ideals that was to become an important characteristic of the Russian revolutionary movement in the second half of the nineteenth century. A systematic thinker of a sort, who anticipated the future in his political ideas, he envisaged the wholesale liquidation of the imperial family, including women and children, as the necessary prelude to the establishment of a totalitarian society with an elaborately organized secret police, espionage, and strict censorship—a society in which all private associations would be banned. Pestel, moreover, developed, and fully approved of, the idea of a temporary or transitional dictatorship and showed considerable awareness of the way in which Russia's social and economic backwardness could be translated into an advantage and exploited as an asset to the revolutionary cause.[7]

The emphasis on social justice, which was to become one of the hallmarks of Russian radical thought, was among the important contributions to the Russian revolutionary tradition made by M. V. Petrashevsky and his followers in the 1840s. Already among the *shestidesiatniki*, the "men of the Sixties," and even earlier among the Jacobin members of Petrashevsky's circle—N. A. Speshnev, V. A. Golovinskii, and K. I. Timkovskii—we find the blind faith in the inevitability and desirability of revolution which is so characteristic of Bolshevism. Lenin's willingness—in fact, eagerness—to employ na-

tionalist traditions for the imposition of a new rational
social order also had echoes in the past, in Pestel, Chernyshevsky, Tkachev, and, to a lesser extent, Herzen and
Bakunin.[8] Lenin's idea of the tutelage state and his
image of communism as "the great school of national
life" had antecedents in the political thought of P. L.
Lavrov. Even Lenin's concept of the "professional revolutionary" had a Russian precedent and model in the
figure of Nechaev and found an early theoretical exposition in the notorious *Catechism of the Revolutionary*
(1869), as well as in the writings of P. N. Tkachev,
the most important theoretician of Russian Jacobinism.
It was Tkachev, finally, who in the 1870s developed
views on revolutionary organization, the nature of the
forthcoming revolution in Russia, and, most important,
a concept of the revolutionary state, which in a striking
fashion anticipated Lenin's political program.[9] In both
Tkachev and Lenin, furthermore, we find the same sense
of urgency—the conviction that the revolution had to be
made "now or never." From this point of view, the
political program of Tkachev's *Nabat*, written in 1875,
and Lenin's letter to the Central Committee of the
Bolshevik Party, written on the eve of the October
Revolution, make for instructive reading.

It was this tradition which fascinated the young
Lenin when he became a revolutionary in 1887. And in
his characteristically thorough way, he learned as much
as possible about the history of the Russian revolutionary
movement, "utilizing every opportunity . . . to absorb
[its] experience." [10] He assimilated the basic ideas and
history of the Russian revolutionary tradition in an os-
mosislike process through his own involvement in the
"order of knights," as N. V. Chaikovskii once described
the revolutionaries. He discovered its spirit and temperament through oral transmission and by studying,

insofar as they were available to him, the writings of the revolutionaries of the past, as well as Plekhanov's *Our Differences*, the first systematic attempt to deal with the Russian revolutionary tradition and the problem of revolution in Russia from a Marxist point of view—a book which was required reading for all revolutionaries of Lenin's generation. Moreover, it was not only during his formative period that Lenin was interested in learning about the history of the Russian revolutionary movement. According to V. Bonch-Bruevich, who helped organize the library and archives of the Russian Social Democratic Labor Party in 1904 in Geneva, Lenin at that time was very much interested in the history of the revolutionary movement in Russia and especially in the "old revolutionary literature." He reports that the Bolshevik leader read "with the greatest care and attention" Tkachev's *Nabat*, the journal *Obshchina*, and Nechaev's proclamations, as well as other revolutionary pamphlets. Lenin was most interested in Tkachev and highly recommended the "rich literature of this original writer" to his followers.[11]

These facts call into question the notion that Lenin's involvement with the Russian revolutionary tradition, and especially with its Jacobin orientation, was a short-lived flirtation, soon replaced by his conversion to Marxism. The evidence, on the contrary, suggests that the imprint of the Russian revolutionary tradition on Lenin was both deep and permanent.

The Impact of Marxism

In assessing the relative importance of Marxism on the formation of Lenin's political thought, one must, first of all, take into consideration the fact that by 1888–89, when Lenin initially became acquainted with Marx, many members of the Russian intelligentsia had turned to this new prophet from the West and a number of Marxist ideas had already become absorbed in the Russian revolutionary tradition. Thus, for example, Tkachev, whose ideas Lenin found so fascinating, professed to be a Marxist—a claim which Soviet historians, with the exception of M. N. Pokrovsky and a few other writers in the 1920s and early 1930s, have generally dismissed, but which has some basis in fact if one considers what Marxism meant in Russia during the 1870s and 1880s.[12]

Secondly, by the time Lenin began reading *Das Kapital*, the Russian soil had been well prepared for the reception of Marxism as a revolutionary doctrine. In his essays in *Sovremennik*, Chernyshevsky, using Aesopian language, had unequivocally stated the case against reform and for revolution—a singularly brilliant performance under the censorship conditions of the time. In his work *The Anthropological Principle in Philosophy*, the former theology student from Saratov had undertaken the exposition of materialism. And in his translation of J. S. Mill's *Principles of Political Economy*, to which he appended extensive critical comments, Chernyshevsky had succeeded in explaining the economic basis of socialism, an accomplishment which earned him the praise of Marx. In 1865 Tkachev had mentioned the name of Marx for the first time in the Russian press, translating a passage from *Zur Kritik der Politischen Ökonomie* and describing this opus by Marx as the first work to express clearly the idea of economic materialism —an idea to which "no intelligent man can find any serious objection." [13] Finally, in 1883 Plekhanov, the "father of Russian Marxism," had published *Socialism and the Political Struggle*—a pamphlet which Lenin later called "the first *profession de foi* of Russian socialism" —followed in 1884 by his famous *Our Differences*.

Lenin's gravitation toward Marxism, therefore, was in many respects quite natural and followed a pattern which characterized the history of the Russian intelligentsia in the nineteenth century. In fact, given the ambiguous legacy of Marxism, anyone who had wrestled with Chernyshevsky's ideas as Lenin had could conceivably find in the Marxist doctrine the confirmation of a good many elements of the Russian revolutionary tradition. What is more, in proceeding from Chernyshevsky to Marx, Lenin once again followed the example of his older brother, who—as Lenin told I. Lalaiants in 1893—had "considered himself a Marxist."

Alexander Ulyanov, as we have seen, had assiduously studied the first volume of *Das Kapital* during his last summer at Kokushkino. At his trial he had spoken of the "historical inevitability with which every country develops toward socialism" and had expressed solidarity with the ideas of social democracy and with Plekhanov's Liberation of Labor Group.[14] In the program of the Terrorist Fraction of *Narodnaia Volia*, which he reconstructed from memory after his imprisonment, he had called for "the nationalization of all land, mills, factories . . . and [other] means of production."[15] Indeed, Lenin's brother had stood at the very crossroad of *Narodnaia Volia* and Marxism in Russia. And thus the search for Alexander led young Lenin not only to Chernyshevsky and practical involvement in the revolutionary movement, especially among the Jacobins and adherents of terrorism, but also to Marxism.

Alexander Ulyanov's interest in Marx is a fact generally known—though the legend of Sasha the non-Marx-

ist terrorist and Vladimir the teen-age Marxist still sur-
vives in the Soviet Union. The nature and full extent of
Alexander's involvement with Marxism, on the other
hand, have remained relatively unknown. Historians and
biographers, for example, have usually overlooked the
fact that Lenin's brother had resolved to undertake a
thorough study of "all the works of Marx and Engels,
beginning with the very first" and had, indeed, begun
such a study.[16] Shortly before his arrest in 1887, he had
translated into Russian a long article from *Deutsch-
Französische Jahrbücher* entitled "Zur Kritik der Hegelschen Rechtsphilosophie. Einleitung" (1844), one of
Marx's earliest writings, which contained much of his
future philosophy in embryo and also, as we shall see,
some essential ingredients of Bolshevism. Probably
through O. M. Govorukhin, a fellow conspirator, Alexander's translation found its way to Geneva, where it was
published, together with a foreword by P. L. Lavrov,
at the end of 1887.[17]

We do not know precisely when and under what
circumstances young Lenin became acquainted with this
"consummate expression of the radical mind," as Robert
C. Tucker has aptly characterized this exceedingly important essay [18] in which Marx for the first time developed the concept of the proletariat. Most likely, Lenin
learned from his mother that his brother Sasha, even
in the face of death, had been concerned about the fact
that the copy of *Deutsch-Französische Jahrbücher* containing the essay by Marx had been confiscated at the
time of his arrest and could therefore not be returned
to V. V. Vodovozov, a fellow student from whom he
had borrowed it. It is also possible that Lenin learned
about "Zur Kritik" from his sister Anna; from I. N.
Chebotarev, who had been Alexander's roommate until

shortly before the assassination attempt; or from Vodo-vozov himself, whom Lenin met in the fall of 1890 during his first visit to Saint Petersburg. In any case, we know from Lenin's *What the "Friends of the People" Are and How They Fight the Social Democrats*, written in 1894, that he was acquainted with this essay by Marx.

It is not difficult to see why this early exposition of Marx's revolutionary credo would appeal to a follower of Chernyshevsky and an admirer of "his merciless polemical talent." Using bitter and sarcastic language, the twenty-five-year-old Marx, still very much under the influence of Saint-Simon when he wrote this essay, declared "war on the status quo in Germany," on its "petrified social conditions," which he considered to be "beneath the niveau of history." He spoke of the German regime as "an anachronism, a flagrant contradiction of generally accepted axioms," an "ancient configuration," mortally wounded and being conducted to its grave by history.

Young Lenin, however, was probably less interested in the scorn which Marx poured on Germany—by Russian standards an advanced and highly civilized country—than in what he had to say about the relationship of ideas to political change and about "practical activity *à la hauteur des principes*, i.e., revolution." Progressive ideas, Marx suggested, are the product of criticism—criticism whose object it is not merely to refute but to strike and destroy. In order to be effective, however, ideas must be harnessed to force. As Marx put it, "the weapon of criticism cannot . . . replace the criticism of weapons, material force must be overthrown by material force."

Most important, in this essay by Marx young Lenin

encountered the idea which was to become of central importance in the Bolshevik theory of revolution—the idea that revolutionary theory "becomes a material force as soon as it seizes the masses." More specifically, Marx suggested that philosophy, i.e., criticism and ultimately revolutionary theory, would find its *"material* weapons in the proletariat," a new class whose very arrival on the historical scene would signal the impending dissolution of the existing social order. In this essay Marx also developed the argument that it would be much less utopian to strive for a *radical* revolution aiming at universal human emancipation than for "a partial, *merely* political revolution which leaves the pillars of the structure intact"—an idea which had also excited the imagination of Tkachev in the 1860s and constituted the basis of his theory of "historical leaps." [19]

Finally, from reading this seminal essay by Marx, young Lenin learned that there is, or should be, a mutual relationship between thought and reality. In the words of Marx, "it is not enough for thought to strive for realization; reality must itself strive toward thought." But the role of thought is clearly primary. Revolution, Marx said in so many words, begins in the brains of philosophers. "Philosophy," he wrote, "is the head of this emancipation," i.e., revolution, which will come about when "the lightning of thought has penetrated thoroughly into [the] naive soil of the people." [20] Here, in embryonic form, is the crucial Leninist idea that revolutionary consciousness does not spontaneously develop in the people, but must be brought to the masses from the outside.

Thus by 1894 all the essential ingredients of Bolshevism were present in Lenin's experience. Yet six more years were to elapse before he would combine these ingredients into the political formula which proved to be so spectacularly successful and singularly consequential in 1917—a formula originally designed for the primary purpose of solving the problem of revolution in Russia, but destined to set the stage for the opening act in the global drama of anti-Western rebellion that has been unfolding before our eyes ever since the end of the First World War.

Bolshevism: The Fusion of Two Revolutionary Traditions

Unlike preceding generations of Russian revolutionaries who were exclusively concerned with the problem of revolution in Russia, Lenin—as Trotsky once correctly observed—came to think of revolution in global terms. However, it was the search for a revolutionary strategy applicable to Russia which led Lenin to adopt the universalistic language and categories of Marxism. Furthermore, Lenin's awareness of the peculiar socioeconomic and political conditions of Russia shaped his understanding and interpretation of Marx in a very fundamental way. Finally, it was the uniqueness of Russia's situation, as perceived by Lenin, which, in combination with his own psychological inclinations and needs as well as his involvement and experience in the Russian revolutionary movement, led him to the formulation of the revolutionary doctrine known as Bolshevism. In short, it was Lenin's changing understanding of the revolutionary situation in Russia, not his varying estimate of conditions in Europe or elsewhere, which was primarily reflected in his intellectual evolution during the years 1887–1900, an evolution which was marked by several distinct stages and which was considerably more complex than has been suggested by most Soviet historians and official biographers of Lenin.

During the first five years of his revolutionary career, from 1887 to 1892, young Lenin, as we have seen, stood under the influence of the terrorist tradition of *Narodnaia Volia*. As Golubeva tells us, he was greatly interested in the problem of the "seizure of power" and questioned neither the feasibility nor the desirability of bringing down the autocracy through a *coup d'état* carried out by a conspiratorial organization of revolutionaries employing terror and any other necessary means. The scenario of revolution envisaged by Lenin at this time included a spontaneous peasant uprising, in the tradition of Pugachev and Stenka Razin, against the autocracy, already weakened and debilitated by a successful campaign of terror.

In 1892–93, under the influence of Marxism and Plekhanov's *Our Differences*, Lenin lost faith in the revolutionary character of the peasantry. He now sought the "material force" of the revolution in the growing industrial proletariat and before long reached a momentous conclusion concerning the revolutionary situation in Russia: he became convinced that capitalism was already a *fait accompli* in Russia, a position which was at variance with the views of both the proponents and the opponents of the idea that the development of capitalism in Russia was inevitable.

Curiously enough, he arrived at this conclusion under the influence of a study of *rural* conditions in southern Russia, published in 1891 or early 1892 by V. E. Postnikov.[21] In this work, whose enormous influence on the formation of Lenin's early political views, as Valentinov correctly points out, most biographers and historians have failed to recognize,[22] Lenin found evidence that the process of "class differentiation" in the Russian village was in full swing and that the exploitation of hired labor by land-owning peasants was a widespread phenomenon in the Russian countryside. While his contemporaries were still debating the vexed question *"Quo vadis,* Russia?" the twenty-two-year-old Lenin had come to the conclusion that "in essence, our order of things does not differ from that of Western Europe." [23]

The problem of the pattern and direction of Russia's socioeconomic, cultural, and political development was an old one in the history of the Russian intelligentsia. In the nineteenth century it had been raised by P. Ia. Chaadaev in his famous *Philosophical Letters* (1836); it had subsequently been debated by the Slavophiles and Westerners in the drawing rooms of Moscow and Saint Petersburg; it had preoccupied the Populists during the 1870s and in 1881 had led to an exchange of letters between Vera Zasulich and Karl Marx.[24]

In the 1890s the question of Russia's future socioeconomic development was one of the cardinal issues dividing the Marxists and the Populists. But whereas Plekhanov and Struve, as well as the other early Russian Marxists, regarded capitalism as a potentially beneficial process that had just begun in Russia, and the Populists warned against the imminent dangers of the growth of capitalism in Russia, Lenin declared categorically that capitalism already existed in Russia. In one of his earliest extant works, written in the autumn of 1893, he spoke of "a quite firmly established and already conceited bourgeoisie" in Russia and argued that "capitalism already at the present time constitutes the basic background of Russian economic life." [25]

The political implications of this analysis—made at

a time when 87 per cent of the Russian population was still classified as rural—were truly stupendous. If capitalism already existed in Russia, then, following Marxist reasoning, the revolutionary calendar called for a socialist revolution and the dictatorship of the proletariat, not for a bourgeois-democratic revolution. Lenin's analysis, in other words, implied the rejection of the traditional and widely accepted two-stage concept of revolution; it implied that Russia was ripe for the kind of ultimate revolution envisaged by Marx in *The Communist Manifesto*.

Moreover, since the defeat of the bourgeoisie, along with the overthrow of the autocracy, was the next order of business, it was not only pointless but even detrimental to the revolutionary cause to continue the quest for political liberty, i.e., the struggle for civil rights and democratic institutions. The liberalization of Russian society would only strengthen the position of the bourgeoisie or, in other words, the enemy. Accordingly, in *What the "Friends of the People" Are*, Lenin termed all demands for political liberalization as reactionary and called on the Russian socialists to make "a full and final break with the ideas of the democrats." [26] At this point in his revolutionary career, then, Lenin for the first time explicitly separated democracy from socialism—a separation which later found expression in his elitist approach to revolution and ultimately became institutionalized in the Bolshevik Party and its successor, the Communist Party of the Soviet Union.

Finally, during this second stage of his intellectual development Lenin became increasingly convinced that the peasantry was bourgeois and reactionary in its outlook and could, therefore, not be relied on to support the revolution. This view may have been a factor in Lenin's refusal to take part in relief efforts organized by members of the intelligentsia in Samara during the terrible famine of 1892. More and more he looked to the industrial proletariat as the "material force" of the revolution even in backward Russia. As a matter of fact, as early as 1894 he had visions of the Russian worker's leading not only the Russian people, but also the proletariat of all other countries *"by the direct road of open political struggle to the victorious Communist Revolution."* [27]

What is important for our inquiry is the fact that, while Lenin began to think of revolution in Marxist terms and categories, he remained a Jacobin by disposition and temperament. Perhaps unaware of the anti-Jacobin views developed by Marx and Engels in their later years, Lenin could very well claim to be a Marxist and Social Democrat, while retaining his belief in the effectiveness of terror as a weapon against the autocracy and continuing to be fascinated by the problem of the seizure of political power.[28] Golubeva reports that during the years 1892–93, when Lenin already regarded himself as a Marxist and Social Democrat, he was nevertheless prone to challenge the "constitutional illusions" of those who professed admiration for German Social Democracy.[29] Indeed, in many respects Lenin may be understood as the embodiment par excellence of the Jacobin spirit and tendency of early Marxism, i.e., Marxism before 1850.

In any event, after six years of active involvement in the revolutionary movement, young Lenin—although temperamentally and psychologically quite different from his brother—had arrived at very much the same point of view as that held by Alexander in 1887. He, too, had now reached the crossroad of *Narodnaia Volia* and Marxism, by then a well-traveled junction. But from here on, after

a short-lived and curious interlude during which he became—at least outwardly—a full-fledged Marxist and Social Democrat, Lenin would blaze his own trail—a trail
which was not anything like the straight, wide, and
brightly lit thoroughfare leading to the October Revolution so often portrayed in Soviet accounts of Lenin, but
which, in the fashion of a narrow and winding mountain
path, took him to the pinnacle of power in 1917.

Lenin did not become actively involved in the revolutionary movement in the capital immediately after his
arrival in the fall of 1893. During 1893–94 he was preoccupied with writing various essays and reviews, none
of which were published. He also wrote some strike
literature and attended Marxist study circles. It was
through one of these circles that Lenin met Nadezhda
K. Krupskaya, who was to become his life companion and
"bride of the revolution," as she has been called in a
recent biography.[30]

The third phase of Lenin's intellectual evolution
began in the fall of 1895 when he returned from his first
trip abroad. Visiting Germany, France, and Switzerland, he had gained a firsthand knowledge of German
Social Democracy, had read an enormous amount of
Social Democratic literature, and had met with both
Akselrod and Plekhanov. During the previous year he
had concluded a working alliance with Peter Struve and
had corresponded with N. E. Fedoseev, an outstanding
young Russian Marxist for whom he had high regard.[31]
All these encounters and experiences had a moderating
and mellowing effect on Lenin, at least for the time
being. When he returned to Saint Petersburg from
abroad, he no longer "turned his back on the liberals," to
use Plekhanov's phrase, but resolved to cooperate with
all opposition elements, including the bourgeoisie, in a

united front against czarism. He now became preoccupied with the problem of organizing a political party in Russia patterned after the Social Democratic Party in Germany. To this end, he took an active part in propaganda and agitation work in the capital. These activities led to his arrest in December of 1895.

Thus, in 1894–95 Lenin seems to have abandoned the idea that Russia was ripe for a socialist revolution. In one of the characteristic tours de force which were to mark his later political career, he now identified the attainment of political liberty as the main goal of the Russian working class. He spoke of a constitution, of universal suffrage and civil rights, and called for the convening of the *Zemskii Sobor,* i.e., a Land Assembly—a traditional demand of Russian revolutionaries.[32] Whereas in the summer of 1894 he had wanted to dissociate democracy from socialism, he now argued precisely the opposite, declaring the struggle for socialism to be inseparable from the struggle for democracy.[33] At this point in his life, he apparently became convinced that Marxism contained the key to the problem of revolution in Russia. In his magnum opus, *The Development of Capitalism in Russia,* written during 1896–99 in prison and exile, Lenin—as Krupskaya wrote in her memoirs—set out to "translate Marxism into the language of Russian facts." One is tempted to speculate how different the world might be today had this been the final and lasting phase of Lenin's intellectual evolution.

In any event, Lenin's activities as a Social Democrat were short-lived. Although—thanks to his good *Narodnaia Volia* training, as Krupskaya put it in her memoirs—he managed to elude the police for several weeks, his attempts to organize the labor movement soon led to his arrest. During the night of December 8–9 (20–21), 1895, the "barrister" Ulyanov was imprisoned for the second time in his life, together with A. A. Vaneev, P. K. Zaporozhets, G. M. Krzhizhanovskii, and others—this time for a period of fourteen months.

During his imprisonment Lenin occupied Cell 193 in the House of Preliminary Detention in Saint Petersburg. The laws and political practices of czarist Russia allowed him to receive food parcels and money from his family. He could ask for mineral water from the pharmacy—"it is brought to me the same day I order it." In a letter to his sister Anna, dated January 12, 1896, he chided her for bringing him such an "immense quantity of bread"; he predicted that the bread would last for "almost a whole week" and would probably get as hard as the "Sunday pies on Oblomovka"—a reference to a scene from Goncharov's novel *Oblomov*. "I am eating very little bread now," he informed her, "and am trying to observe a certain diet."

There was a prison library, and on Wednesdays and Saturdays his sister Anna would bring him the books he requested from the libraries of the Academy of Sciences, the university, and the Free Economic Society. As in the case of his earlier exile at Kokushkino, Lenin put his enforced idleness to good use by beginning his important and longest work, *The Development of Capitalism in Russia*. He exercised regularly each evening before going to bed, doing about "fifty prostrations" in rapid succession "without bending the knees." He read "fiction for relaxation" and communicated and even played chess with his fellow prisoners by means of a code of knocks for the letters of the alphabet. He slept well—about nine hours a day—"dreaming about various chapters of my future book." According to the unpublished memoirs by his brother Dimitri, cited in the June, 1963, issue of *Novyi mir,* Lenin left his cell almost with regret when he was released from prison on February 17 (March 1), 1897: "If I had been in prison longer, I would have finished the book."

After fourteen months in prison and a series of interrogations, Lenin was sentenced to three years of exile in Siberia. Prior to his departure into exile, however, he received five days of liberty in Saint Petersburg, which he promptly used to resume his contacts with the revolutionary movement, and four days in Moscow during which he stayed with his family. He then went into exile as a free man and at his own expense, an option which the practices of autocratic Russia accorded to most political prisoners. On the way he stopped for five weeks in Krasnoyarsk, where he spent most of his time doing research in the famous Yudin library, which in 1907 became an important component of the Slavic Collection of the Library of Congress in Washington, D.C.

Until February 1900, Lenin lived in exile in Shushenskoe, a village on the River Shush, not far from the right bank of the mighty Yenisey and the town of Minusinsk. The picturesque surroundings of his place of exile—Shu-shu-shu, as he affectionately referred to it in his correspondence—induced Lenin to try his hand at poetry: "In Shush, at the foot of the Sayan [Mountains.] . . ." But he never got beyond this first line, as he confided to his mother in a letter written on May 8, 1897. He had complete freedom of movement, traveled miles from the village in pursuit of duck and snipe, swam in the Yenisey in the summer and went ice-skating in the winter. He corresponded with socialists in Russia and Europe and received letters, periodicals, and books from abroad. "Today I received a pile of letters . . . from all corners of Russia and Siberia," he wrote to his mother on February 24, 1898, "and therefore felt in a holiday mood all day." He sent endless lists of requests to his family—a mackintosh cape, some socks, a suit, "my straw hat, if it is still in existence," a pair of kid gloves to wear in the summer as protection against mosquitoes, newspapers, the classics of political economy and philosophy, a pencil (Hardmuth No. 6), and some paper *ruled in squares.* For the eight rubles a month which the government allowed him, he received, in the words of Krupskaya, "a clean room, board, laundry and mending service." Although as an exile he had no right to do so, Lenin even practiced law, giving free legal advice and assistance to the peasants and settlers in the area. "The Minusinsk district was liberal in those days. Actually there was no supervision at all."

In exile, Lenin was joined by Krupskaya, his fiancée, who had been arrested in 1896 for organizing a strike and had subsequently been exiled for three years to the northern Ufa province, but had received permission to join Lenin on condition that they marry immediately. Although the emotional involvement of the partners to this marriage seems to have been minimal in the beginning, they soon developed genuine affection for one another, and the marriage lasted in spite of the very considerable strains to which it was subjected at various times.

There is some evidence that Lenin had failed at an earlier attempt at courtship and marriage. He had apparently proposed to Appolinaria Yakubova, who—like Krupskaya—was a schoolteacher and a member of a Marxist study circle in Saint Petersburg, but was rejected. After his marriage to Krupskaya, Lenin at one time became very much attached to Inessa Armand, a fellow Bolshevik of striking appearance, lively intellect, and refined cultural tastes. He was deeply affected by her death in 1920. However, Lenin did not let this passionate interlude interfere with his marriage or his vocation as a revolutionary. He managed the relationship with discretion—though Krupskaya knew about it—and, as Angelica Balabanoff, an eyewitness, relates in her memoirs, from Inessa's funeral he "went straight back to his desk."

Considering the circumstances of Lenin's life, his relationship to Krupskaya seems to have been, on the whole, surprisingly harmonious and normal. Their inability to have children was apparently a source of great regret to Lenin, who had fond memories of his own childhood and throughout his life remained deeply involved with the members of his parental family. The pattern of intellectual collaboration and joint effort on behalf of the revolution was established at the very beginning of their marriage. Immediately after their wedding on July 10, 1898, the newlyweds began translating *The History of Trade Unionism* (1894) by Sidney and Beatrice Webb, and before long Krupskaya was transcribing the chapters of *The Development of Capitalism in Russia* that poured from Lenin's pen.[34]

During the last year of his exile, Lenin's conviction that he had found in Marxism the guidepost to revolution in Russia was severely shaken by the emergence of two "heresies" among Russian Marxists, economism and revisionism—heresies which soon became confused in his mind. In the late 1890s, i.e., during the period of Lenin's imprisonment and exile, the Russian working class had experienced rapid growth. Under the leadership of its own intelligentsia it soon became an independent force, preoccupied with the pursuit of its own immediate interests, namely, the improvement of its economic position, and growing increasingly immune to the influence of the few agitators and radical intellectuals remaining at liberty. In other words, the Russian working class was moving toward trade unionism, not toward revolution. Faced with the prospect of losing all contact with the proletariat, some socialist intellectuals in late 1897 openly called for a postponement of the political struggle and support of the workers in their quest for economic gains. The "economists," as they came to be called, wanted the Russian Socialists to support the immediate goals and interests of the workers, viz., higher wages and shorter working hours, and—in the field of politics—to endorse the demands of the liberals for a constitution and the introduction of Western political institutions in Russia.

Moreover, in early 1899 a number of leading Russian Marxists, following the example of E. Bernstein in Germany, began to express doubts about the feasibility of a social revolution. Struve, for example, called for an extensive critical appraisal of Marxism.[35]

If, from Lenin's vantage point, economism was an infectious disease threatening to attack the Marxist organism, revisionism represented a danger on the order of the medieval Black Death. And of all places, the plague broke out in Germany, the country which at the time seemed to offer the brightest prospects for the establishment of Social Democracy; the country in which Socialism had not only survived the Anti-Socialist Laws of Bismarck, the Iron Chancellor, but—like many a religious faith under similar circumstances in the past—had actually grown stronger; the country in which the Socialists constituted a political force, both in the *Reichstag* and outside, with which even the all-powerful Junker class and the emperor had to reckon. But the growing material and political prosperity of the German

Socialists was matched by a decline in revolutionary activity and spirit. While in official programs and pronouncements the German Social Democrats continued to adhere to the revolutionary doctrine of Marxism, German Social Democracy was, in fact, becoming more and more bourgeois. It was only a matter of time before someone would point out the need to bring theory in line with practice and the facts.

Nevertheless, when E. Bernstein in 1888–89 did just this, arguing that such main tenets of Marxism as the increasing misery of the proletariat under capitalism had been clearly refuted by history and should be abandoned, the effect was that of a bombshell. And Bernstein did not stop there! His argument culminated in a more or less open call to abandon the revolutionary side of Marxism, its determinism, its pretension and claim to be a scientific system of thought. Continued adherence to revolutionary Marxism, he pointed out, would deprive the Social Democrats of the support of potential allies, especially the middle class—support which they needed in order to attain their goals, namely, social reform and a steady improvement of living conditions, as well as the increasing democratization of German society. The reverberations of Bernstein's doctrine of evolutionary socialism throughout the Marxist world were multiplied by the realization that his analysis was basically irrefutable and by the fact that Bernstein, along with Karl Kautsky, was one of the most respected and revered Socialist leaders, a man who had been Friedrich Engels's close friend and literary executor, a man, moreover, whose intellectual honesty and integrity were recognized by Socialists everywhere.

Lenin's initial reaction to these developments was surprisingly mild and cautious [36]—the proverbial calm before the storm. But when in July of 1899 he received a copy of the economist *Credo* [37] from his sister Anna, followed a month later by Bernstein's explosive book, *Die Voraussetzungen des Sozialismus und die Aufgaben der Sozialdemokratie,* he was greatly alarmed. Krupskaya's memoirs suggest that Lenin now went through a real crisis: he "suffered from insomnia and grew terribly thin." [38] It was this crisis which resulted in the birth of Bolshevism.

As the end of his exile approached, Lenin became more and more preoccupied with the diagnosis of the ills and "disorders" that afflicted the Social Democratic movement. He now became as profoundly disillusioned with the industrial proletariat as he had earlier with the peasantry. According to Krupskaya, his thoughts increasingly focused on the problem of the "correct Social Democratic leadership of the party." Sometime in the autumn of 1899 he reached the conclusion that the Achilles heel of the Social Democratic movement was its inadequate organization. "We must openly admit," he wrote in late 1899, "that in this regard we lag behind the old Russian revolutionary parties. . . ." He called for "the improvement of revolutionary organization and discipline" and "the perfection of our conspiratorial techniques" as an absolute necessity for any progress in the labor movement.[39] Lenin was beginning to waver in his commitment to Social Democracy—and once again it was the maelstrom of the Russian revolutionary tradition which proved irresistible.

In the closing days of the nineteenth century, when the Social Democratic movement in Russia showed every sign of impending disintegration, Lenin, in an essay entitled "Urgent Questions of Our Movement," formulated the basic principles of Bolshevism. Separated from

Social Democracy and correct leadership, he concluded, "the labor movement degenerates and inevitably becomes bourgeois." The function of the Social Democrats, therefore, was not merely to assist the workers, but to guide and direct them, *"to inculcate socialist ideas and political self-consciousness into the mass of the proletariat* and to organize a political party inseparably linked with the spontaneous labor movement." This task, he argued, could be accomplished only by full-time, professional revolutionaries, "men who devote to the revolution not only their free evenings, but their whole life." [40]

Implicit in this analysis is the assumption that revolutionary consciousness is the exclusive prerogative of the few, that the masses—the peasantry as well as the proletariat—are basically conservative, and that democracy in the labor movement leads to reaction, not to revolution. In Lenin's proposed solution to this problem, the perspectives of the Russian revolutionary tradition increasingly reasserted themselves, perspectives which in 1900 perhaps no longer reflected the political realities of Russia as accurately as they had in earlier decades. Lenin's prescription for party organization was virtually identical with that of Tkachev, and in his concept of the "professional revolutionary" we can recognize many attributes of Chernyshevsky's Rakhmetov and the fanatic, totally dedicated "doomed man" described in Nechaev's sinister *Catechism*. Indeed, during the years ahead, Lenin himself, like no other man before him, was to become—in the words of Karl Radek—"the personification of the will to revolution." [41]

4
THE QUEST FOR POWER

The year 1900, as Lenin himself recognized, marked the end of a period in his life, a period during which he had believed in the possibility of cooperating with the liberal bourgeoisie and in the practicality of fusing the idea of democracy with the idea of social revolution. In a note to himself, penned at 2:00 A.M. on December 29 of that year, after yet another exhausting negotiating session with the "democratic opposition," i.e., P. B. Struve, Lenin revealed that he realized he had come to a crucial turning point in his political career. He spoke of the end of an epoch and noted that the negotiations with Struve had been of historic significance in his life, "determining . . . [its] course for a long time to come." [1]

Having earlier rejected the peasantry and the industrial proletariat as unreliable allies, he now broke with the liberals as well and returned to his pre-1895 position, once again regarding the bourgeoisie as an essentially reactionary class. His break with the liberal elements in Russian society became final in the spring of 1901. In an essay entitled "The Persecutors of the *Zemstvo* and the Hannibals of Liberalism," written in June of that year, he attacked liberalism and especially Struve, who during the previous year had left the ranks of the Social Democrats and joined the liberals—an act which henceforth earned him the pejorative "Judas" in Lenin's correspondence. [2]

Lenin had now reached a point in his revolutionary development at which the question was no longer one of finding new allies—by 1900 he had tried them all and found them wanting—but one of creating and properly organizing a revolutionary force capable of destroying the autocracy. In other words, he had come to the conclusion that the revolutionary forces furnished by history were not equal to the task or not good enough. Like Zheliabov, his famous predecessor, he was determined and ready to give history a push, to fashion his own instrument of revolution.

The Spark

Already during his last year in exile Lenin had conceived the plan of an all-Russian newspaper, whose purpose it would be to create a unified, disciplined and centralized revolutionary party. Following the example of Herzen's *Kolokol*, Lavrov's *Vpered*, and Tkachev's *Nabat*, the paper was to be published abroad and smuggled into Russia. Taking as its motto a line from the Decembrist Odoevskii's reply to Pushkin, the newspaper *Iskra* was to be the "spark" which would "kindle the flame" of revolution. Above all, the function and purpose of *Iskra* was to "facilitate the political development and the political organization of the working-class," to strengthen the connection between it and Russian Social Democracy, "the vanguard in the struggle for political liberty."

Lenin's revealing and prophetic lead editorial, published in the first issue in December 1900, hammered away at themes which would dominate his thinking from now on: the need for leadership and organization, the necessity of organizing a political party capable of waging "a determined struggle against the autocratic government and the whole of capitalist society." He spoke of the inherent tendency of the proletariat to lose its political independence and become bourgeois—a tendency which could be overcome only by the conscious guidance, direction, and leadership of the masses by the vanguard of professional revolutionaries, who represent "the interests of the movement as a whole [and] point out to this movement its ultimate goal, its political tasks." Acknowledging all methods of struggle to be admissible, as long as they were practical and realistic, he held out the vision of a single strike turning into a political victory over the government and a revolt in a single locality growing into a victorious national revolution. This prescription for imminent political change on a grand scale in Russia resounded with echoes of Tkachev and Bakunin, but contained precious little of Marx. And significantly, the editorial concluded with a quotation from a speech by Petr Alekseev, a Russian revolutionary of the 1870s, predicting that the "yoke of the autocracy will be smashed into atoms . . . [by] the working millions." [3]

In contrast to the majority of his contemporaries and most revolutionaries, Lenin was in many respects a very pragmatic man. This fact in itself goes far in explaining his success as a revolutionary and political leader. While there was a strong utopian element in his thought —a topic to which we shall return later—this utopianism was constantly tempered by practical considerations and an awareness of limits, by a pragmatism rarely found among revolutionaries. One is struck by the fact that among Lenin's voluminous writings one does not find a single work that was not motivated by an immediate, practical problem. Whatever Lenin may be said to have been, he does not qualify as a philosopher or speculative thinker. His most important philosophical work, *Materialism and Empiriocriticism*, like all his other writings, was inspired by "serious political circumstances"— to use Lenin's own words [4]—viz., to inflict a crushing blow on his political opponents, including A. Bogdanov, a philosopher who played a key role in such practical matters as procuring funds for the party. In other words, Lenin's writings reflected, above all, the changing realities of the revolutionary situation in Russia as he perceived them, and frequently his own immediate environment and experiences.

Reading the vast literature written by Lenin after 1899, one is impressed, on one hand, by his practical turn of mind, his generally sober analysis of often unpleasant facts, his tactical flexibility and ability to maneuver; on the other hand, one is struck by the persistent presence of a strong utopian element in his thought—an element which is usually submerged and overshadowed by his pragmatic concerns of the moment but which surfaces again and again, by a certain psychological rigidity, by a narrowness of thought which stands in sharp contrast to his exceptional intellectual abilities, and by the extent to which he remained a prisoner of his time and the circumstances surrounding him. Perhaps most forceful and compelling is the impression that by 1900 Lenin had reached a plateau: for twenty-one years, from the turn of the century to 1921, his intellectual development, as it were, essentially came to a standstill.

In the years following his exile in Siberia, Lenin became totally preoccupied with fighting the twin dangers of economism and revisionism. All his activities, as well as his intellectual endeavors, during the years 1900 to 1903 were related to this central concern. Characteristically, he gave vent to his scorn and outrage in a stream of articles bristling with vituperative language. He now developed the complex of ideas which found its supreme expression in *What Is to Be Done?* and which has gone down in the annals of history as Bolshevism—a revolutionary doctrine that was poles apart from his "economist" position in 1895. No longer did he believe that "the struggle of the workers . . . for their daily needs of itself and inevitably forces the workers to think about questions of the state and politics . . ." and that the task of the revolutionaries consisted of "helping the workers in this struggle which they themselves have already begun to fight." [5] On the contrary, he made it clear that what was needed was a general staff of the revolution, a group of professional experts who would do the thinking for the masses, organize them into an effective fighting force, and at the appropriate moment lead them into battle. Only such a force, uniting the awakening proletariat with all other revolutionary elements in Russian society and led by the revolutionary elite, could hope to win the decisive battle with the autocracy and "capture the fortress . . . which is raining shot and shell upon us, cutting down our best fighters." [6]

The practical counterpart to this theoretical struggle of the pen against economism and revisionism was Lenin's attempt, together with A. N. Potresov, J. O. Martov, Plekhanov, Akselrod, and Zasulich, to unite the Russian revolutionary movement around *Iskra*, the newspaper which had come into being after protracted and difficult negotiations at the end of 1900. Perhaps no episode in Lenin's life better illustrates his ability and willingness to subordinate his personal feelings to the interests of the revolutionary cause than the history of the birth of *Iskra*. When in August of 1900 he came to

Geneva to secure the collaboration of Plekhanov and the Liberation of Labor Group in the publication of *Iskra*, he, like Potresov, was subjected to the most humiliating and insulting treatment by Plekhanov, the high priest of Marxist orthodoxy, whom Lenin had idolized from afar for many years and whom he greatly admired at the time because of his uncompromising rejection of Bernstein's revisionism. As Lenin himself put it, he had been "blindly in love" and "infatuated" with Plekhanov. Now his idol treated him with incredible condescension and even contempt for having made overtures and concessions to Struve.

In a most revealing document, Lenin left us a record of the negotiations and an account of how his "infatuation" with Plekhanov "vanished as if by magic." Still under the immediate impression of what had happened, he wrote: "I felt offended and embittered to an unbelievable degree. Never, never in my life had I regarded anyone with such sincere esteem, respect, and veneration; never had I 'humbled' myself so completely before any man—and never had I been so brutally 'kicked' [and] . . . trampled underfoot." [7]

Yet, as he gained some distance on the encounter with Plekhanov and recovered his sober frame of mind, he concluded that it would be "entirely unreasonable to give up the enterprise." Undoubtedly, he realized that he could never hope to unify the Russian revolutionary movement without the help of Plekhanov or to publish an all-Russian newspaper without his collaboration. As so often in the past, personal feelings were suppressed in order to proceed with the business at hand. Cemented by their common desire to preserve "orthodox" Marxism and to reject anything that smacked of economism or revisionism, the incongruous alliance of the two men survived until 1903, the year in which Lenin split the Russian Social Democratic movement into Bolsheviks and Mensheviks.

What Is to Be Done?

and the "Orthodox" Revision of Marxism

While Lenin, like the revolutionaries of the 1870s, failed to realize his dream of unifying the Russian revolutionary movement, he put the years 1900 to 1903 to good use. On the one hand, he waged a bitter struggle against the more moderate trends in the Social Democratic movement then emerging in Russia. On the other hand, during the long years of emigration—from 1900 to 1917 Lenin lived for the most part in Munich, London, Paris, "accursed Geneva," and elsewhere in Western Europe, moving at times to Poland, Finland, and Austrian Galicia, returning to Russia only briefly in 1905—he patiently built up inside Russia the kind of centralized, conspiratorial party which he regarded as necessary for the success of the revolution, an enterprise in which he was ably assisted by Krupskaya, who joined him in exile abroad in 1901 and became secretary of the *Iskra* organization. Carried on behind the backs of his colleagues on the editorial board of *Iskra,* this activity—in a kind of parallel to the Hague Congress thirty years earlier—culminated in the split of the Russian Social Democratic Labor Party at its Second Congress in London.

Most important, in March 1902 Lenin published his most famous political pamphlet, *What Is to Be Done?*—the crowning achievement of his theoretical efforts and his practical revolutionary activity. This "crude little book," as Robert C. Tucker once described it (in a lecture dealing with the unique place of *What Is to Be Done?* in the history of political thought and its significance as one of the most important books of the twentieth century), contained the blueprint of the party organization which in 1917 would "overturn the whole of Russia" and subsequently become the key element in the political structure of Soviet Russia. Written primarily for a Russian audience and reflecting the seemingly unique conditions of the Russian revolutionary situation, the pamphlet had a significance not generally recognized at the time. Although some of Lenin's contemporaries sensed that a new page had been turned over in the history of Russian Social Democracy, no one—Lenin included—realized that in the twentieth century this unique polemical tract was destined to become the textbook for both Marxist and non-Marxist political movements seeking to destroy liberal democracy.[8]

What Is to Be Done? was not only a "symbolic title" for Lenin's entire literary activity and a work whose "theoretical basis . . . is a preliminary thesis of his whole world outlook," as George Lukács has observed,[9] but it also signified his drive to become the undisputed leader of the Russian Social Democratic movement. In choosing the title of Chernyshevsky's novel for his most important political pamphlet, Lenin, addressing himself to a generation of Russian revolutionaries which had not yet forgotten the famous editor of *Sovremennik*, acknowledged his own intellectual debt to the leading radical of the 1860s and laid claim to his throne and mantle of spiritual leadership in the Russian revolutionary movement.

Chafing under the "dictatorship" of Plekhanov[10] and feeling increasingly isolated even among his colleagues on the editorial board of *Iskra*, Lenin was ready to play for high stakes. *What Is to Be Done?* was the beginning of the end of his collaboration with Plekhanov, Akselrod and Martov. With fifteen years of theoretical training and practical experience in the Russian revolutionary movement behind him, Lenin was prepared to take the first crucial step in his bid for power. The political program which he developed in *What Is to Be Done?* may be interpreted as the product of his determination to stake everything on his ability to remake the Russian Social Democratic Labor Party in his own image and his faith that his interpretation of Marxism would ultimately prevail.[11]

On the surface, *What Is to Be Done?* appeared to be a critique of economism and revisionism, the two heresies of Social Democracy as perceived by Lenin. Underneath, the future bible of Bolshevism was nothing less than an attempt to revise Marxism and bring it up to date, with special reference to conditions in Russia. Unlike Bernstein and Struve, however, Lenin did not admit his revisionism. On the contrary, he proclaimed his position to be that of orthodox Marxism. Yet, as Adam Ulam has put it, "by any objective standard, Lenin revised the doctrine of the Master as much as Bernstein did." [12]

Marx had regarded revolutionary class consciousness to be the natural and spontaneous product of the life experience of the working class. Lenin, by contrast, concluded that "class political consciousness can be brought to the worker *only from the outside.*" Without the assistance of the revolutionary intelligentsia, he argued, the working class could develop only "trade-union consciousness." He cited Karl Kautsky in support of his central thesis that "socialist consciousness is something which must be carried into the proletarian class struggle from the outside" and categorically denied that the labor movement by itself was capable of developing an independent ideology.[13]

As a matter of fact, Lenin assigned a rather unimportant and inferior role to the workers in the history and development of socialism. Marx and Engels had been members of the intelligentsia, he pointed out, and socialism had grown up "quite independently . . . of the labor movement." In Russia, too, Social Democracy had come into existence "as the natural and inevitable result of the ideas" and dreams of the revolutionary socialist intelligentsia.[14]

But while the revolutionary intelligentsia in *What Is to Be Done?* clearly emerged as the primary force in the struggle for socialism, Lenin also expressed his disenchantment with its contemporary representatives. He accused his political opponents of having committed "the fundamental error" of "subservience to spontaneity" and spoke of the failure of the Social Democrats to realize that spontaneity of the masses demands mass consciousness on the part of the revolutionaries. The weakness of the movement, in short, lay in "the lack of consciousness and initiative among the revolutionary leaders." The working class, he argued, was far more revolutionary than the intelligentsia supposed, and dissatisfaction with the existing order was widespread in Russian society. The problem was to transform these isolated forms and expressions of discontent into the conviction that "the whole political system is worthless," to combine and organize all the existing revolutionary forces in Russia, these "drops and streamlets of popular agitation," into "a *single* gigantic flood" of revolution.[15]

In 1899 Lenin had rejected the accusation that he, along with Plekhanov and others, was trying to turn the

Socialist Party into "an order of 'right believers' which would persecute the 'heretics.'" [16] Three years later he was determined to "draw firm and definite lines of demarcation" between the small group of select revolutionaries who, "surrounded by enemies," were moving "along a precipitous and difficult path" toward revolution and "the inhabitants of the swamp," i.e., the economists, revisionists, and other critics of Social Democracy. Calling for a complete "change of the tactics that have prevailed in recent years," he began the process of doctrinal reduction, compression, and narrowing that was to have such fatal consequences for Russian Social Democracy fifteen years later. In the preface to the first edition of *What Is to Be Done?*, he quoted with approval Lassalle's statement to Marx that diffuseness in a party is a sign of weakness and that a party becomes stronger by purging itself. In the text of the pamphlet itself, he spoke in ominous and prophetic terms of the necessity "to settle accounts with the other trends of revolutionary thought, which threaten to divert the movement from the correct path." [17]

The collective hero of Lenin's *What Is to Be Done?*, it goes without saying, is the party, whose upper-echelon members share many of the attributes of Chernyshevsky's "new men." Ascetic in their personal life, fanatic in matters of doctrine, totally dedicated to the revolutionary cause, these "real leaders" and "tribunes of the people" constituted the active priesthood of the new militant faith, the "religion without a God," to use Churchill's phrase, which in 1917—in the name of the ideals of the French Revolution—would inaugurate the age of totalitarianism.

Expressing his faith in the "miracles" that can be performed by the energy of small circles and even individuals in the revolutionary cause, Lenin sketched the outline of his party of professional revolutionaries which would "dictate a positive program of action" and inculcate in the workers "genuinely political consciousness," i.e., train them to develop "a Social Democratic response, and not one from any other point of view." Guided by the "most advanced" scientific theory—for "without a revolutionary theory there can be no revolutionary movement"—the party would lead the Russian proletariat not only to victory over the autocracy, but also to a place of honor among the workers of the world. Once again, Lenin held out the vision of the Russian proletariat's inheriting the mantle of leadership from the German Social Democrats and becoming "the vanguard of the international revolutionary proletariat." [18]

Stressing the uniqueness of the revolutionary situation in Russia in an argument which recalled Tkachev's polemic with Engels in 1874,[19] Lenin explained at length why a democratic party was not possible in Russia and why "broad democracy" in a revolutionary party was "a useless and harmful toy." The special conditions of Russia called for a party organized on the basis of conspiratorial principles, with a hierarchical command structure, a high degree of discipline and centralization, and a limited membership. Indeed, only a party of professional revolutionaries would be a match for the czarist secret police.

Without completely denying the role of the masses in the revolutionary struggle, Lenin expounded a clearly elitist conception of revolution—a conception which breathed the spirit of Chernyshevsky and Tkachev. And indeed, *What Is to Be Done?* is full of references to the Russian revolutionary tradition! "Our cardinal sin in regard to organization," Lenin wrote, "is that *by our primitiveness we have lowered the prestige of revolutionaries in Russia."* He made it clear that he regarded Alekseev, Myshkin, Khalturin, and Zheliabov as heroes. He referred to Herzen, Belinsky, and Chernyshevsky as the "predecessors of Russian Social Democracy" and spoke with admiration of the "brilliant galaxy of revolutionaries of the 1870's" and their "magnificent organization . . . which should be a model for all of us." [20]

Thus the elitist political party, inspired in its organizational principles and functional purposes by the Russian revolutionary tradition, emerges as the *deus ex machina* in Lenin's political thought. "The whole of political life," he wrote, "is an endless chain made up of an infinite number of links. The whole art of politics consists of finding and getting a firm hold of that link which is least likely to be torn out of your hands, which at the given moment is most important and which best guarantees control of the whole chain." [21] Unlike most of his fellow revolutionaries, Lenin recognized that the "key link" controlling the whole of political life was the state and that an elitist and highly disciplined political party would be the most ideal instrument for "getting a firm hold" of that vital link in the chain of political life. During the long years of underground struggle, exile, and party polemics, he never lost sight of the importance of political power. In this emphasis on "first things first," Lenin was the uncontested heir of Tkachev, who in the 1870s had for the first time in the history of the Russian revolutionary movement unequivocally stated the case for the primacy of politics, arguing that the social revolution must be preceded by the seizure of political power. And again like Tkachev, Lenin perceived that a conspiratorial and elite party of professional revolutionaries would be the pivotal element in the revolutionary struggle for the destruction of the old and the construction of the new society. To the professional revolutionaries would fall the role of architects in the revolution. The workers would be the "bricklayers" who would build the structure—without having seen or understood, let alone approved, the master blueprint for the new society.

The reaction to Lenin's newest revolutionary scripture was not long in coming. After the London Congress of 1903, which marked the beginning of the split in Russian Social Democracy and laid the foundation for the emergence of two separate political parties in 1912, Lenin was subjected to a constant stream of criticism by his former political comrades-in-arms. Trotsky called him a despot and terrorist and accused him of wanting to transform the Central Committee of the party into a "Committee of Public Safety" in order to become a new Robespierre. In a prophetic assessment published in 1904,[22] the future chairman of the Petrograd Soviet and founder of the Red Army predicted that Lenin's centralistic conception of the party would inevitably lead to the degeneration of the dictatorship of the proletariat into the dictatorship of one man—a prognosis which was echoed by the Menshevik Martynov. Lenin was also criticized by Rosa Luxemburg and Akselrod, who spoke of the Jacobin and "theocratic" character of his conception of the party.

Whenever Lenin learned of these criticisms, he flew into a rage and turned into a "tiger," ready to attack his critics by the throat. Generally speaking, however, he showed remarkable restraint in his public relations with them. As Edmund Wilson has suggested, the impression that Lenin became "the victim of a theological obsession with doctrine" is superficial. It was only when ideological disputes assumed practical political significance in his eyes that Lenin knew no limits. Thus, for example, it was not until Struve had outlived his usefulness and emerged as a potentially dangerous political opponent that he became for Lenin "a traitor, renegade, Judas, and new Tikhomirov," who "ought to be killed." [23]

Lenin himself was the living example of a strange contradiction: on the one hand, he attacked the Populists, economists, and revisionists in the name of orthodox Marxism and showed considerable reluctance to tamper openly with basic Marxist doctrine or to admit his own revisionism; on the other hand, he demonstrated remarkable tactical flexibility in questions of ideology, treating Marxism not as a dogma but as "a guide to action." As we have seen, in *What Is to Be Done?* he revised the Marxian theory of revolution in important points, injecting into it a strong voluntarist element which reflected the influence of the Russian revolutionary tradition and in effect negated the determinism of the Marxist doctrine, at least in its post-1850 formulation.

Lenin's book *Imperialism as the Highest Stage of Capitalism*, written in 1916, was yet another example of an attempt to revise essential elements of Marxism without explicitly abandoning the Master's teachings. Drawing freely and without full acknowledgment on the ideas of Hobson, Hilferding, Luxemburg, and Bukharin, Lenin, in his theory of imperialism, tried to explain the unpleasant fact that the revolution predicted by Marx had not yet taken place in any of the advanced capitalist countries. Obviously something was wrong with Marx's prognosis: more than two generations after the publication of *The Communist Manifesto* not a single proletarian revolution had taken place. But instead of abandoning Marxism or openly admitting the need to reexamine some of its major premises, Lenin explained the unexplainable. Capitalism, he said, had managed to escape its inherent contradictions temporarily by expanding its search for cheap labor and raw materials, as well as new markets for its products and excess capital, to the whole world. Without realizing its theoretical implications fully at the time, Lenin developed an analysis of economically backward societies which differed in important details from that of Marx and ultimately led to the conclusion that the revolution was more likely to happen (or easier to accomplish!) in underdeveloped countries.

More specifically, his theory of imperialism attempted not only to explain why the revolution predicted by Marx had not yet taken place, but also to prove the ultimate inevitability of that revolution. However, whereas Marx had thought of the revolution within the context of Western Europe, Lenin thought of it in terms of global perspectives. He accepted the Marxist analysis of capitalist society and the theory that capitalism must, and will necessarily, lead to crises and revolutionary situations; but he extended this analysis to the noncapitalist, underdeveloped part of the world as well. For Lenin it had become self-evident that the whole world had been turned into one gigantic market for capitalist expansion and exploitation, that the entire globe had become, as it were, a single capitalist-imperialist society beset by all the contradictions which Marx had found in his analysis of "classical" capitalism. Imperialism, in short, was capitalism on an international scale and level.

Whereas Marxism in its theory of revolution had clearly focused on the advanced industrialized countries of Western Europe, Leninism increasingly developed into a doctrine of revolution whose motto could be described as *ex oriente lux.* In a new "dialectics of backwardness," as A. G. Meyer has called Lenin's attempt to improve on Marx's theory of historical development, the author of *Imperialism* stressed the uneven development of capitalism and the worldwide coexistence of states in different stages of socioeconomic development. In a backward society, Lenin reasoned, especially one which comes into active contact with an advanced civilization, all the contradictions and strains endemic to capitalism are exacerbated. In the epoch of imperialism it was possible for backward nations to inherit and take over advanced Western developments and ideas, to adopt the most radical political ideologies originating in an industrialized society, and thus to become carriers of an advanced social—i.e., "proletarian"—consciousness.

Once again silently revising the Master's teachings on a crucial point, Lenin concluded that Marx had been wrong in postulating a direct correlation between the level of socioeconomic development and the evolution of radical political ideas. The exact opposite was true. *Ceteris paribus,* the highly industrialized societies will tend to be *status quo*-oriented; it is the economically backward nations, suffering from the domination and exploitation of the advanced countries, which tend to be most inclined toward rebellion against the existing order. In short, revolution is not likely to occur in countries where capitalism is highly developed, but in countries where it is still in the state of infancy.

It is this aspect of Lenin's thought—somewhat sporadically and not always clearly or consistently developed over a period of several years—which, together with his voluntarism and his ambivalent attitude toward industrial capitalism, made his version of Marxism so attractive to national leaders in underdeveloped countries. In Lenin's theory of imperialism, the characteristic Marxist ambivalence toward modern industry and technology is elevated into an ambivalence toward the West. To put it differently, Leninism can be interpreted as a doctrine of economic development for the sake of national emancipation and independence, and, in a larger sense, as a doctrine of Westernization or modernization for the sake of anti-Western rebellion.

Thus, in Lenin the idea of socialism became fused with the idea of nationalism, resulting in an entirely new and different theory of revolution. The class struggle of *The Communist Manifesto* became merged with the struggle between nations pictured in *Imperialism*. In 1920 Lenin went so far as to suggest that the Marxist slogan "Proletarians of all countries, unite" had become obsolete. Henceforth it should read: "Proletarians of all countries *and oppressed nations*, unite." [24] As the events of the past decades have shown, the man from Simbirsk, whose ancestry, social origin, life history, and intellectual evolution were in many ways symbolic of the revolutionary intelligentsia in underdeveloped countries today, had hit upon an exceedingly potent political formula.

The postulation of the universal goal of economic development for the sake of national liberation—irrespective of the presence or absence of native cultural affinities supporting such development—*ipso facto* presupposed the use of politics, ideology, and pedagogy of the masses, i.e., what Marx had called the "superstructure." Economic determinism was conveniently forgotten or overlooked. As a matter of fact, Lenin's political program tacitly acknowledged the primacy of politics over economics, of consciousness over socioeconomic existence. From this stance it was only a step to the development of Leninism as a theory of the revolutionary state.

The State: Target and Instrument of the Revolution

In Russian political thought one finds an interesting and significant ambivalence concerning the concept of the state. On the one hand, there is the extremely negative attitude, epitomized perhaps in the Russian Orthodox ideal of *otserkvlenie*,[25] in the conviction of the Old Believers that the Russian state was the embodiment of Antichrist, in Dostoevsky's vision of a universalized Orthodox Church, and in Tolstoy's passive anarchism; on the other, there is the imputation to state authority of a sacred mission—an idea which reflects the influence of Byzantine thought, the concept of political power as a kind of theurgical instrument, and the confident and frequently unqualified defense of political authority, in particular the autocracy, by such men as M. V. Lomonosov, I. T. Pososhkov, and K. P. Pobedonostsev. This characteristic ambivalence was fully reflected in Russian revolutionary thought of the nineteenth century and found its supreme expression in Chernyshevsky, as well as in his most famous pupil, V. I. Lenin.[26]

Writing in 1875, Tkachev had defined the primary problem of revolution as the conversion of the *conservative* state into a *revolutionary* state. A generation later, Trotsky expressed his belief that the state is an entity capable of pursuing different and even diametrically opposed social goals and objectives. He wrote in 1906: "The state is not an end in itself, but is a tremendous means for organizing, disorganizing, and reorganizing social relations. It can be a powerful lever for revolution or a tool for organized stagnation, depending on the hands that control it." [27] Lenin, too, while committed to "smashing and destroying" the existing bourgeois state, firmly believed in the potential utility of the state as an instrument of revolution and social change. His theory of revolution, which was Marxist in form but not in content, called for the replacement of the existing political order by the "dictatorship of the proletariat," i.e., "the organization of the vanguard of the oppressed as the ruling class." [28] Unlike Marx, however, who thought of the dictatorship of the proletariat as the political hegemony of the majority over its former exploiters, established gradually through "winning the battle of democracy," [29] Lenin conceived of the dictatorship of the proletariat as the rule of the revolutionary segment of society over its nonrevolutionary elements.[30]

Once again following in the footsteps of Tkachev, Lenin insisted that the revolutionary vanguard must have complete control over the state after the overthrow of the old order. He wrote on the eve of the October Revolution: "The doctrine of the class struggle, as applied by Marx to the question of the state and of the socialist revolution, leads necessarily to the recognition of the *political rule* of the proletariat, its dictatorship, i.e., of power shared with none. . ." [31]

Apparently oblivious, or indifferent, to the fact that the Marxian concept of the dictatorship of the proletariat, when applied to Russia, of necessity meant minority dictatorship, Lenin, in a striking and prophetic passage in *The State and Revolution*, revealed just how imperative the possession of state power is for the success of the revolution: "The proletariat," he wrote, "needs state power, the centralized organization of force . . . [and] violence, in order to suppress the resistance of the exploiters and to *lead* the great mass of the population—the peasants, the petty bourgeoisie, and the semi-proletarians—in the 'establishment' [*nalazhivanie*] of a socialist economy." [32] In other words, Lenin, too, believed in the possibility of utilizing the vast power of the state for the attainment of revolutionary ends; indeed, the idea of the revolutionary state emerged as a crucial element in his theory of revolution.

Lenin's pamphlet *The State and Revolution* has frequently been dismissed by historians and biographers as an "aberrant intellectual enterprise," a "monument to its author's intellectual deviation during the year of revolution, 1917," as not much more than an "exercise in daydreaming." [33] This interpretation, it seems to me, is open to question. It fails to recognize, *inter alia*, that underneath Lenin's pragmatism as a revolutionary there was always a powerful utopian vision—a vision that sustained him even during the darkest and most despairing days of his underground and exile existence. Though frequently submerged and perhaps eclipsed by his political pragmatism, the presence of a utopian element in Lenin's political thought can be demonstrated in his writings as far back as 1894. [34]

During most of his adult life Lenin was preoccupied with the problem of how to make a revolution in Russia. Like most revolutionaries, he gave relatively little thought to the precise circumstances and details of life after the revolution. But in 1916 and early 1917, at a time when he doubted that his generation would live to see "the decisive battles of . . . [the] coming revolution," [35] he sketched the outlines of the future, postrevolutionary society in *The State and Revolution*, his "secret last will and testament," according to Trotsky.

Originally entitled *Marxism on the State* and essentially completed before the October Revolution, [36] *The State and Revolution* was largely based on Marx's *The Civil War in France*, a work in which Marx had advanced a dubious interpretation of the Paris Commune of

1871, "the first manifestation of a real proletarian revolution." The central message of Lenin's celebrated pamphlet—which had begun as a critique of N. Bukharin and developed into an attack on Karl Kautsky, written explicitly for the purpose of "restoring the true doctrine of Marx on the state"—was that a successful proletarian revolution would lead to the establishment of a stateless and classless society, a society characterized by rationality, perfect equality, social harmony, and justice. After a period of proper social and psychological conditioning, the people, in the higher stage of communism, would voluntarily subordinate their individual interests and desires to the needs of the whole society. Man's competitive spirit would disappear in the presence of material abundance for all. Everybody would naturally and voluntarily "observe the fundamental rules of social life." Consequently, there would no longer be a need for any type of coercion. The state would lose its *raison d'être* and "wither away," as Engels had predicted.[37]

The utopianism of *The State and Revolution* provides a striking contrast to the stark realism of *What Is to Be Done?* As a matter of fact, the spirit of the two works is difficult to reconcile. In many respects, *The State and Revolution*—with its anarchist tendencies, its emphasis on the spontaneous abilities and key role of the masses in the construction of the new society, as well as its concomitant de-emphasis of discipline and organization (the party is mentioned only once, peripherally!) —seems to be the perfect antithesis of the elitist and managerial approach to revolution which constitutes the central theme of *What Is to Be Done?* Yet the disparity is only superficial. In developing his utopian vision of the new society, Lenin expressed his belief—typical of the radical mentality—in the ultimate rationality and perfectibility of man, as well as his conviction that these inherent characteristics and attributes of man had been distorted and suppressed by the existing forms of social organization, in particular by the state. Moreover, in a sense, the utopianism of *The State and Revolution* is a measure of Lenin's indebtedness to European socialism, in particular Marxism, and the Russian revolutionary tradition: it fully reflected the ambiguity of the Marxian concept of the state and the ambivalence of Russian political thought in regard to *gosudarstvo*, i.e., the state, and it affirmed the faith of Godwin, Bakunin, and Marx in the possibility of the total regeneration of man— a faith also shared by Chernyshevsky and Tkachev.

In contrast to *What Is to Be Done?*, Lenin's *The State and Revolution* was not so much concerned with the practical politics of the immediate present as with the theoretical exposition of the future society under socialism. However, while clearly the most utopian of all his writings, *The State and Revolution* was not without pragmatic significance. Once the new society became a matter of practical politics after the Bolshevik *coup d'état* in 1917, Lenin, as we shall see, would abandon many of the ideas elaborated in *The State and Revolution*. But to the end of his life he remained under the spell of the apocalyptic assumption that—after the destruction of the existing socioeconomic and political order in the purgatory of the revolution—a new harmonious, egalitarian, and just society could be built by the revolutionaries through the systematic, rational, and unlimited use of political power, the ultimate goal supposedly being the abolition of any and all forms of political authority and the creation of a new stateless society. What is more, the formative period of the Soviet political regime, as we shall see, stood clearly under the influence of the ideas which Lenin had developed in *The State and Revolution*.

5

SUCCESS AND FAILURE

Unlike most revolutionaries, whose ideas suffer the proverbial fate of the storm in the teacup and whose names are more or less quickly relegated to the sidelines of history, V. I. Lenin was destined to leave a deep and permanent imprint on his own age and on generations to come. The October Revolution not only shook Russia to its very foundations, but also sent shock waves throughout all Western Europe and Asia. Most important for our inquiry is the fact that the successful seizure of power by the Bolsheviks in the second Russian Revolution of 1917 placed Lenin in a position to put his political ideas into practice—an opportunity rarely given to revolutionaries. In the postscript to the first edition of *The State and Revolution,* written on November 30 (December 13), 1917, Lenin informed his readers that the writing of the pamphlet had been interrupted by the political crisis leading to the October Revolution. He welcomed this interruption and declared that "it is more pleasant and useful to go through the 'experience of revolution' than to write about it." [1] And thus the second part of his famous pamphlet, which was to have dealt with "The Experiences of the Russian Revolutions of 1905 and 1917," was never written. Instead, Chapter VII of *The State and Revolution* was, as it were, dictated to life—life with all its complexities, its frequently incomprehensible contradictions, its recalcitrance and refusal to be forced into a passive role, its tendency to destroy noble ideals by the baseness of human existence, and its habitual inclination to correct lofty theories by the practical limitations of reality. When Lenin dictated the "continuation" of *The State and Revolution* in the form of governmental decrees, he was no longer writing alone. For the first time in his thirty-year-long career as a revolutionary he had acquired a powerful and obstinate coauthor, life itself—a coauthor who would soon wrest the pen from his tiring hand.

Preludes to October

The revolutionary wave in the twentieth century which was to bring the Russian autocracy to its knees and carry the Bolsheviks into power in 1917 began in January 1905. After the disastrous Russo-Japanese War of 1904, mutiny in the army, and a series of political assassinations of czarist officials and ministers—met with indifference by Russian society—the autocracy was literally sitting on top of a volcano. Respect for law and order was at an all-time low. When V. K. Pleve, the Minister of the Interior, was assassinated by a Social Revolutionary in 1904, even members of the nobility greeted the news with joy. Feelings of national shame combined with a growing sense of outrage at the persistent refusal of the czar and his reactionary entourage to grant a constitution and elementary political rights regarded as normal in every civilized state. By 1905 the striving for political freedom had become almost universal, permeating all segments of Russian society.

The eruption was not long in coming. When on January 9, 1905, czarist troops fired on unarmed men, women, and children peacefully demonstrating in Saint

Petersburg and attempting to present a petition to their emperor, the workers throughout Russia responded with strikes and violence. In the cities, "soviets," i.e., workers' councils, sprang up spontaneously, at first as strike committees, later as organizations promoting insurrection. From the large cities, the revolutionary movement spread to all corners of the empire: there were nationalist demonstrations in Warsaw, unrest in the army, and disturbances in Odessa and at the naval base in Sevastopol. Perhaps the single most dramatic incident, immortalized in Eisenstein's famous film, was the mutiny on the *Potemkin*, a battleship in the Black Sea.

In some respects, the Revolution of 1905 may be regarded as a dress rehearsal for what was to happen twelve years later. Certainly it contained many of the ingredients that went into the making of the February and October Revolutions of 1917: a disastrous military defeat, peasant unrest, strikes and workers' demonstrations, and general hostility toward the established political authority even among the educated classes. But in 1905 the revolution was elemental, unorganized, and anarchist in character. None of the political parties had much influence on the course of events or succeeded in placing itself at the head of the revolution.

The role of the Bolsheviks and Lenin in the events of 1905 was negligible. Lenin did not return to Russia until November, i.e., not until after the government had declared an amnesty as part of the concessions it made in an attempt to curb the spirit of the revolutionary movement. On his arrival in Russia, Lenin was shocked by the lack of preparedness of the Bolsheviks. He chided them for not having manufactured any bombs. Without becoming actively involved himself, he preached frantic violence and direct action, going into great detail about how to kill policemen, how to use guns, knives, kerosene, bombs, and boiling water. Yet, Lenin, too, failed to develop a coherent program of action. Pretending that the Bolsheviks were actually leading the revolution, he declared in September 1905 that they stood for the confiscation of the large landed estates, that they would never tie their hands, and that they would organize revolutionary committees consisting not only of workers, but also of peasants, paupers, soldiers, and prostitutes.

The czarist government's response to the 1905 Revolution was a policy of alternate reforms and repressions. On October 17 (30), 1905, the government finally granted a constitution. But at the same time, it did not hesitate to exploit the violence and anarchy which the Revolution had produced. During 1905 to 1907 hordes of reactionary hooligans, the infamous *chernosotentsy* or Black Hundreds, conducted a campaign of terror against university students, liberals and revolutionaries. Some government officials were so unscrupulous as to turn the violent anti-Semitism latent among the Russian population into political advantage: anti-Jewish pogroms were officially condoned (and even encouraged and instigated), especially in the eastern and southern parts of European Russia. By the end of 1905 the Revolution was effectively over, although it did not run its full course until 1907.

After 1905 Lenin faced an entirely new situation. Russia now had a parliament (*Duma*)—albeit one based on an unsatisfactory and increasingly narrow franchise. Revolutionaries, including Bolsheviks, could be—and were!—elected to the *Duma*. Opposition newspapers and periodicals could now be published in Russia. In short, the conditions of illegality which had been Lenin's justification for insisting on a secret and conspiratorial organization of revolutionaries no longer prevailed. Yet there was no essential change in Lenin's views on party organization. When the Mensheviks succeeded in pushing through the reunification of the Social Democratic Labor Party at the Fourth Party Congress in Stockholm in April 1906, Lenin submitted—and immediately proceeded to organize a secret Bolshevik "center." He continued his vitriolic attacks on the Mensheviks, *inter alia* falsely accusing them of having entered into a conspiracy with the liberal Constitutional Democrats. While at one time he publicly endorsed the idea of a unified mass party, he never abandoned his conviction that a secret revolutionary organization was absolutely essential, and he pursued his drive for such an organization with singular determination and relentlessness.

Twelve years later, when Lenin was once again living in Switzerland, history repeated itself, surprising the Bolshevik leader with the outbreak of the February Revolution of 1917. Largely in response to food shortages and a rapidly growing inflation, partly for political and patriotic reasons, ninety thousand textile workers went on strike in Petrograd, as Saint Petersburg was called from the outbreak of the First World War until 1924, when it was renamed Leningrad. Within twenty-four hours, the ranks of the strikers had swelled to two hundred thousand. When the city's garrison refused to assist the police in restoring order and in some instances even fired on the police, the riots assumed the dimensions and character of a revolution.

Confronted by these events and faced with the refusal of his army officers to support him, the czar, who at the time was at the headquarters of the Northern Group of Armies in Pskov, abdicated. More than three hundred years of continuous rule by the Romanov dynasty came to an end. For the next eight months Russia, still at war with Germany, had no central government. The disintegration of the autocracy led to the establishment of two governments: the Provisional Government, appointed by an executive committee of the *Duma* and headed first by Prince Georgi Lvov, who was succeeded in July by Alexander Kerensky; and the Petrograd Soviet of Workers' and Soldiers' Deputies, which—though it represented at most only the capital—claimed to speak for all workers and soldiers in Russia.

Like the Revolution of 1905, the February Revolution took the political parties in Russia, including the Bolsheviks, by surprise. In January 1917, Lenin had told a group of Swiss students that "we of the older generation may not live to see the decisive battles of this coming revolution." His initial reaction to the February Revolution was to dismiss it as a plot of the Allies designed to prevent the czar from making a separate peace with Imperial Germany. Understandably, Lenin had trouble comprehending the fact that the masses alone, without guidance from a revolutionary elite, had made a genuine revolution.

Before long, however, he developed a more realistic view of the events in Russia. Eventually, he correctly recognized the February Revolution as national—a revolution which reflected strong patriotic sentiments and the dissatisfaction of the masses with the inability of their government to carry a popular war to a successful conclusion. As he followed the developments in Russia, he grew increasingly apprehensive about his inability to influence the course of events. His apprehension and eagerness to be on the scene turned into frenzy when he learned what was happening to the Bolsheviks in

Russia. It was 1905 all over again! The members of his party were contemplating reunification with the Mensheviks and, what was worse, Stalin and Kamenev, who—after returning from exile in Siberia—were the senior Bolshevik leaders in Russia, were even making conciliatory overtures to the Provisional Government.

Through the mediation of Dr. Alexander Helphand (Parvus), a native Ukrainian and member of the Russian Social Democratic Party, who had coauthored the "theory of permanent revolution" with Trotsky and became rich as a German war speculator specializing in the dissemination of subversive propaganda within the Russian Empire, Lenin arranged with the German government for transit through Germany in the famous "sealed train." General Erich Ludendorff himself, the chief strategist of the German General Staff, approved the transport of Lenin and his comrades via Germany, Sweden, and Finland to Russia, although he did not know in 1917, as he admitted twenty years later, what Lenin actually stood for.

Lenin arrived at the Finland Station in Petrograd on April 3 (16), 1917, and was met by members of his party, a military guard, and assorted "Menshevik scoundrels." The band had not yet mastered the "International," so Lenin had to settle for the "Marseillaise." The fact that this originally revolutionary anthem had become tinged with imperialism, notably that of Napoleon Bonaparte, who a century before had invaded Russia, did not matter. Formalities and protocol did not yet have the significance in the eyes of the Bolshevik Party which they were destined to acquire only a few years later in the eyes of the "revolutionary" government. In his welcoming speech, the commanding officer of the honor guard expressed the hope that "Citizen Lenin" would soon join the Provisional Government!

It goes without saying that nothing could have been farther from Lenin's mind. In his famous *April Theses,* delivered in two speeches on the following day, he began his decisive intervention in the course of the Revolution. He left no doubt in the minds of his listeners that reunification with the Mensheviks was out of the question. He categorically rejected any thought of cooperation with the Provisional Government and stunned his opponents and followers alike by calling for "all power to the soviets." While no longer advocating an immediate peace, he recommended intensive antiwar propaganda among the frontline troops and their fraternization with the enemy. When the *April Theses* were published on April 7 in *Pravda,* they caused a storm of indignation. The Bolshevik Party itself appeared to come apart at its seams—*inter alia,* Lenin had demanded that henceforth his party call itself "Communist," the *coup de grâce* to any hope for the reestablishment of a unified Social Democratic Labor party.

Many people at the time believed that the *April Theses* amounted to political suicide, that after their proclamation Lenin was politically finished. For the *Theses* not only repudiated the prevailing notion of the two-stage revolution and the previous Bolshevik position but, in the eyes of most Russian Socialists, including many Bolsheviks, were tantamount to a rejection of Marxism. There was general agreement among the Russian Marxists that Russia was not yet ready for a socialist revolution, that the 1917 Revolution had to be a bourgeois-democratic one.

As in the case of so many other party crises, however, Lenin did survive. In July of 1917 the Bolsheviks staged their first and unsuccessful attempt at a *coup d'état* under the pretense of a "peaceful demonstration" —featuring twenty thousand pro-Bolshevik sailors from the Kronstadt naval base in full battle dress and carrying rifles. Again, Lenin was unable to give them any directions other than to be vigilant and "all power to the soviets." The attempted coup failed, and after the "July Days" the political fortunes of the Bolsheviks declined temporarily. The Bolsheviks, and specifically Lenin, were accused of having received large sums of money from the German government—a charge since substantiated by the publication of documents from the archives of the German Foreign Ministry. Lenin himself denied the charge—and, to be on the safe side, went into hiding in Finland.

It was not until October 25, 1917—November 7 by the Western calendar—that the Bolsheviks succeeded in seizing power. Taking advantage of the growing disintegration of the czarist empire and the increasing feebleness of the Provisional Government, they simply occupied the most strategic points in the capital and—to use Adam B. Ulam's apt expression—"picked up power." The claims of Soviet historians notwithstanding, the Bolshevik victory in October 1917 was neither a spectacular accomplishment, nor can it be *exclusively* attributed to the political genius of Lenin. With industry in a state of paralysis, anarchy in the countryside, hundreds of competing political authorities, a large part of European Russia under enemy occupation, and more than two million deserters roaming through the country, it took only a handful of determined men to seize power in the capital. And while the *coup d'état* was undertaken at the insistence of Lenin—ever since September he had urged the Central Committee that *now* was the time to act!—the actual preparations were carried out by Trotsky, who had joined the Revolution in May after his release from Canadian internment had been secured by the Provisional Government. Lenin himself did not emerge from hiding and join the Bolshevik headquarters until the night of October 24, i.e., the very eve of the second Russian Revolution in 1917. Important though his role in the October *coup d'état* was—it can be, and has been, argued that without Lenin there would have been no second revolution (or a very different one)— a much better and fuller measure of Lenin's political genius is his success in overcoming the obstacles to Bolshevik power and in conquering the anarchy which he himself had done so much to create.

In Power

Already the Revolution of 1905 had been a powerful stimulus to Lenin's revolutionary optimism—an optimism that found telling reflection in his writings of that period and lingered in his later works, interrupted at various times by moods of acute depression and pessimism. Revolutions, he wrote in *Two Tactics of Social Democracy* (1905), were "the locomotives of history," as Marx had put it, "festive occasions for the oppressed and the exploited," singular historical opportunities which enable "the masses of the people . . . to come forward as . . . the active creators of a new social order," times when "the people are capable of performing miracles." [2] The 1905 Revolution, Lenin said in 1917, had "transformed dozing Russia into a Russia of the revolutionary proletariat and the revolutionary people." [3] Similarly, the immediate effect of the success of the Bolshevik *coup d'état* and the initial euphoria of the October Revolution, as might be expected, was to bring out the utopian element in Lenin. However, instead of writing theses and political programs, engaging in party polemics and disputations with his political opponents, he was now writing decrees—decrees which, at least in some localities in European Russia, soon had the force of law and affected large numbers of people. Having earlier in the year alienated many Russian Social Democrats by the radicalism of his *April Theses* and his resolute defense of the Zimmerwald antiwar platform,[4] he now offered land to the peasants, peace to the soldiers, and "control over production" to the workers in a series of anarchist decrees penned in the full expectation that communism was "just around the corner." Recalling the honeymoon of the Revolution from the perspective of 1921, Lenin admitted that during the winter of 1917–18 "we proceeded . . . from the assumption—perhaps not always openly expressed, but always tacitly taken for granted— . . . of a direct transition to the construction of socialism."[5]

Lenin's utopianism during the months following the Bolshevik victory, however, was not merely, or even primarily, a manifestation of the postrevolutionary euphoria then generally prevailing in Bolshevik circles; it also revealed a great deal about his inner motivations—his consuming desire to transform Russian society fundamentally, to destroy Oblomovism once and for all, to create the kind of social order which Socialists everywhere envisaged in their dreams. It was the vision of an ideal and perfect society which animated and excited the imagination of Lenin throughout his adult life. In pursuit of this vision, he reduced his private life to an absolute minimum, denied himself—in Rakhmetovlike fashion— the pleasures of life, and persuaded, cajoled, coerced, and liquidated others. To Lenin, power was not an end in itself but merely a means—a means for revolution. He never used power for personal advantage (insofar as, in the case of Lenin, personal can be distinguished from political!), preserving his modest life-style even after he had become the most powerful man in Russia. He used power in order to realize his vision of the ideal society—an ideal which always remained out of his reach and has proved equally elusive to his followers.

It was not long, however, before the political realities confronting Lenin's fledgling regime dictated the abandonment of these utopian expectations, at least for the time being. Lenin and his followers now learned the hard and bitter lesson that it is infinitely more difficult to carry out and actualize a revolutionary program than to compose one. Having overthrown the Provisional Government of Alexander Kerensky and seized power, the Bolsheviks found out how ill-prepared they were for the next step and how little Marxism had to offer in the way of a blueprint and concrete, practical guidelines for the building of a socialist society. As Louis Fischer has aptly put it, the Bolsheviks had embarked upon a "journey without a Baedeker." In the confused and hectic months following October 25 (November 7), 1917, Lenin literally "groped his way in the dark," relying on his intuitive judgment in meeting crisis after crisis, engaging in the kind of conduct he had anticipated in a strangely prophetic note scribbled into the margin of von Clausewitz's classic treatise *On War*, a book he had studied with great care in 1914 or 1915.[6]

Even Lenin, with his remarkable self-control and ability to adapt himself to changing demands and circumstances, could not make the transition from revolutionary to *de facto* head of state—disrupted and chaotic though that state was—without experiencing a feeling of dizziness. Shortly after the Bolshevik seizure of power in Petrograd, when he had not even had time to change his collar, he confided to Trotsky in an intimate moment that the sudden change from a life of persecution and underground existence to a position of power made his head swim, using the German expression *"es schwindelt"* [*sic*] and making the sign of the cross.[7] Before long, however, he had grown used to his new role as Chairman of the Council of People's Commissars. During the ensuing months, when his regime was still in its infancy, when crisis followed upon crisis and things continually seemed to go from bad to worse, Lenin developed the full measure of his tactical dexterity.

In the face of necessity, Lenin, like most revolutionaries and many political leaders of more moderate persuasion, showed no compunction. He borrowed the land-reform program of the Social Revolutionaries, the traditional foes of the Bolsheviks, who enjoyed the support of the peasant majority, and openly admitted that he had done so, pointing to the adoption of the SR program by his party as evidence of the "complete and sincere readiness of the Bolsheviks to form a coalition with the vast majority of the Russian population." [8] Initially, Lenin still deferred to the Constituent Assembly as the ultimate political authority. He spoke of his desire to establish a state "always under the control of public opinion" and showed his willingness to make overtures to his political opponents. All too soon, however, his earlier separation of democracy from socialism in the realm of theory was followed by a similar dissociation in practice, with infinitely greater consequences.

For nearly a century Russian liberals and revolutionaries had worked for a constitutional assembly or *Zemskii Sobor*, i.e., a Land Assembly that would draw up a constitution for Russia. After the February Revolution, elections to such an Assembly were set for November 25 by the Provisional Government. Although the Bolsheviks anticipated defeat, they could not very well call off the elections because prior to their successful seizure of power they had claimed that the Bolsheviks alone could ensure that such elections would be duly held. After his return to Russia, Lenin himself had endorsed the idea of a Constituent Assembly. Popular interest in such an election was so great that even after the Bolshevik seizure of power, at the Second All-Russian Congress of Workers' and Soldiers' Deputies on November 8, Lenin had felt compelled to declare in public that the Bolsheviks would yield to the popular masses if they were outvoted in the elections.[9] And so it was that the only free election in Russian history was held on November 25 to 27, 1917, under the auspices of Lenin's regime.

Out of a total of nearly 40,000,000 votes cast, the Bolsheviks received 9,562,358, compared with 17,490,837 votes for the Social Revolutionaries. Clearly, the Bolshevik Party—at the time consisting of approximately 25,000 members—had gained considerable popularity, especially in the industrial centers and in the army, and, most important of all, among the soldiers closest to the capital and to Moscow. But while half of the country voted for socialism, it also voted against Bolshevism.

Lenin now conveniently forgot his promise of November 8. When the elections to the Constituent Assembly revealed the full extent of the weakness of the Bolsheviks in relation to their political opponents—the Bolsheviks received 24.7 per cent of the vote or 175 seats out of a total of 707, as compared to 410 seats for the Social Revolutionaries [10]—and the Constituent Assembly emerged as a potential rival for political authority, as a rallying point and forum for political opposition to the Bolsheviks, Lenin simply torpedoed it by ordering its dissolution. Following the maxim *divide et impera*, which he had used so successfully in dealing with political opposition in the Russian Social Democratic movement before the Revolution, he succeeded in splitting the SR party and concluded a temporary alliance with the Left Social Revolutionaries. This alliance, too, was only a tactical maneuver. When the Fifth All-Russian Congress of Soviets met on July 9, 1918, the Left Social Revolutionaries suffered the fate of all the other political parties that had existed at the time of the Revolution. They found themselves excluded from the soviets, i.e., the workers' councils, at the local, provincial, and national level. The soviets in turn were increasingly fashioned into obedient instruments of the Bolshevik Party. Thus, nine months after the beginning of the October Revolution, which had been undertaken in the name of democracy and freedom, Russia became a one-party state. The outlines of the political order of the first Communist state became visible. Even before the Revolution was one year old, the mold of the future Soviet political system had begun to set.

Measured by any standard, the odds against the political survival of Lenin and his regime were staggering. Along with the war, the Bolsheviks inherited an acute nationalities problem from czarist Russia, as well as a host of other problems. In a minority and isolated at home, they found themselves surrounded by a capitalist world which, though temporarily divided against itself, was united in its opposition and hostility to the new revolutionary regime and before long would resort to military intervention in its attempt to put an end to the "Communist menace" in Russia. The Treaty of

Brest-Litovsk, concluded in March 1918, deprived the Bolsheviks of the most advanced and fertile regions of the former Czarist Empire, including the Baltic, the Ukraine, and Poland—a vast area inhabited by more than one-third of Russia's population. In addition, the Soviet government was forced to cede the frontier districts of Kars, Ardahan, and Batum to Turkey. Had the "Tilsit Peace," as Lenin called the Treaty of Brest-Litovsk, not been annulled by the collapse of Imperial Germany, it would have pushed the western frontiers of Russia back to where they had been in the middle of the seventeenth century and would have effectively reduced her to the status of a second-rate power.

Moreover, in addition to the disruption and chaos produced by War Communism, as the initial period of Soviet rule came to be known, and the Civil War, which brought Russia close to a complete breakdown, Lenin had to cope with opposition within the ranks of his own party on major policy issues. Thus, for example, a powerful group of Bolsheviks, including N. Bukharin, E. Preobrazhensky, A. M. Kollontai, Inessa Armand, Karl Radek, Iu. Piatakov, and many others who played a key role in the party, as well as the two most important party organizations in Russia, i.e., in Moscow and Petrograd, opposed the idea of concluding a peace treaty with imperialist Germany and argued for a revolutionary war.

Yet, in spite of the unfavorable odds, Lenin's regime survived. And that it did is in no small measure creditable to the tactical dexterity and pragmatism of the man from Simbirsk, whose stature in the party and in the government soon eclipsed the position of all other Soviet leaders, including Trotsky. In insisting on negotiating a peace settlement with Germany and ultimately accepting the humiliating Treaty of Brest-Litovsk,

Lenin clearly deviated from his political program of 1915, which had called for a revolutionary war against the capitalist world.[11] And Trotsky, in supporting Lenin's refusal to launch such a war, temporarily abandoned his theory of permanent revolution. But in so doing, both men also demonstrated their realism and pragmatic assessment of the situation. During his first trip to Brest-Litovsk, Trotsky had noticed that the Russian trenches "were almost empty," and Lenin, with his unfailing political instinct, realized that the Russian soldier had voted against the war with his feet. The fate of the Revolution in Russia being at stake, both Lenin and Trotsky were willing to trade space for time. While the ideological goals and revolutionary ideals were not forgotten,[12] they were increasingly eclipsed by considerations of *raison d'état*.

The collaboration between Lenin and Trotsky is one of the most fascinating and intriguing human aspects of the 1917 Revolution. It is eloquent testimony to the emotional commitment of both men to revolution that, after years of polemics and ideological struggle, they were willing to put aside their past differences. Although Lenin disliked Trotsky, he recognized his abilities and his indispensability to the Revolution. A brilliant writer and able theoretician, a flamboyant personality, ambitious, vainglorious, and at times theatrical, Lev Davidovich Bronstein-Trotsky, the son of a Jewish farmer in the Ukraine, possessed a rare talent for organization and was unequaled as a revolutionary orator and agitator. As Commissar of War and founder of the Red Army, as well as in various other capacities, with practically carte blanche authority from Lenin, he made a uniquely important contribution to the survival of the Bolshevik regime.

Lenin's acceptance of Trotsky, as of anyone else, was always limited. After the Civil War he carefully circumscribed the political influence of the Revolution's most romantic and, in many ways, most appealing figure. By contrast, Trotsky's acceptance of Lenin after the October Revolution was unqualified. He came to regard Lenin as the man who would make the world revolution. Until his assassination by a Stalinist agent in Mexico, Trotsky retained his boundless admiration for the man whom before the Revolution he had scorned for his dictatorial ways.

There is evidence that during the initial months of the Revolution Lenin himself rated the life expectancy of his regime very low. He is reported to have been jubilant when he realized that his government had been in existence for seventy-three days, one day longer than the Paris Commune of 1871, after which—at least in theory—it was modeled. Many years before the October Revolution, Lenin had established two conditions for the successful transition to socialism in Russia: the support of the peasantry at home, and the support of a revolution in Europe. Throughout 1917 and early 1918 the Bolsheviks, Lenin included, insisted that the survival of the Soviet regime depended on the realization of these two conditions. However, the much-hoped-for revolution in Europe did not materialize, and before long the Bolsheviks faced not only the sullen obstruction of the peasantry but also passive opposition among the urban workers. The survival of the Soviet regime under these circumstances, which were soon exacerbated by the Civil War and foreign intervention, is a measure of Lenin's political genius. Yet mere political survival does not add up to statesmanship. As we shall see, Lenin ultimately failed to attain the objectives he had set out to achieve—a fact which he himself recognized in 1923 —largely because he was unable to free himself from some of the concepts and thought patterns he had acquired as a revolutionary.

Considering the adverse circumstances surrounding the origin and early life history of the Soviet regime, it is not surprising that Lenin relied so heavily on the instrument which he had fashioned many years before for an entirely different purpose, namely, the Bolshevik Party. Originally conceived as an underground revolutionary party and consciously designed for the purpose of overthrowing the existing political order, taking into consideration the unique features of the revolutionary situation in Russia, the Bolshevik Party, as a result of the October Revolution, was transformed overnight into the ruling party of the largest country in the world and was charged with the task of building a socialist society in an underdeveloped country—a task that, aside from being forbidding in its dimensions, involved very different problems from those which had confronted the Bolsheviks before the Revolution. Yet, in spite of the dramatically changed situation of the Bolsheviks after the October Revolution, Lenin essentially held on to his conception of a highly centralized, tightly organized and disciplined political party, with a narrow membership,[13] a quasi-military *modus operandi*, and a leadership composed more or less exclusively of "professional revolutionaries." The Bolshevik Party, in fact, became the embryo of the new political order which evolved in Russia after the Revolution and which, through its organizational principles, its exclusiveness, its intolerance, and its generally presumptuous mentality, decisively shaped the contours of the future Soviet political system.

The prerevolutionary elitism of Lenin's party, originally justified on the grounds of the threat posed by the czarist secret police, was carried over *in toto* into the postrevolutionary era. But it was not only vis-à-vis the non-Bolshevik segment of Russian society—i.e., a little over 75 per cent of the Russian electorate in 1917—that Lenin's party developed a paternalistic and undemocratic posture. Inner-party democracy, too, received the *coup de grâce* under Lenin. While as Chairman of the Council of People's Commissars Lenin preferred to rule through the *kollegiia* system, i.e., a collegial form of decision making, he did not hesitate to impose his will on the party by threatening to resign. Increasingly Trotsky's celebrated prophecy, dating back to the time when he was sharply critical of Lenin's dictatorial ways, became an accurate description of party life: "the organization of the party takes the place of the party itself; the central committee takes the place of the party organization; and finally the dictator takes the place of the central committee."

Natural and expedient though Lenin's reliance on this kind of party may have been, it deprived his government of the advantages which ultimately accrue from recognizing and dealing with an organized political opposition: *inter alia*, a potentially wider base of legitimacy and support, as well as a more realistic and feasible political course. Lenin, as it turned out, could not escape the mold into which he had forced himself during the long years of exile and underground struggle. He remained a lifelong polemicist and had difficulty learning the art of compromise. He failed to understand that he could not rule the Soviet state by the same methods which he had used to run his revolutionary party. Above all, he was unable to recognize that he could not manipulate Russian society as he had manipulated his party and at the same time hope to develop the mutual trust between the ruled and the rulers which is the foundation and *conditio sine qua non* of any kind of civilized government. Thus, in spite of his impressive political achievements—the masterful handling of the Left Social Revolutionaries and the Constituent Assembly, the neutralization of the nationalities by a contradictory, yet effective, policy of concessions and coercion (granting autonomy in theory, but not in fact), the survival of the Soviet regime against seemingly insurmountable odds—Lenin in the end was a failure as a statesman. And this failure, it may be argued, was rooted in some of the very attitudes and qualities that had enabled him to become such a successful revolutionary leader.

The End of a Dream

It is interesting to conjecture how the Soviet political system might have evolved had Lenin never written *The State and Revolution* and thus not committed himself in advance on the question of the nature of government in a socialist society. Perhaps the contradiction between theory and practice, between official image and reality, would not have developed so sharply during the first year of Soviet rule, and the Bolsheviks would not have felt compelled to force the people to believe in a fiction, thus removing one important factor which propelled the young Soviet regime toward an imperfect kind of totalitarianism from the very beginning.

Once the "real teachings of Marx on the state" had become part of the Leninist canon, however, it was difficult to abandon them. And even though it was possible to ignore the basic tenets of *The State and Revolution* in practice, the Bolshevik regime could not do so openly without undermining its own legitimacy in the eyes of its followers. Thus the stage was set for the basic divergence between the official image of the Soviet political order and the reality it represented—a divergence which has been a permanent and distinctive feature of public life in the Soviet Union ever since the Revolution and which, though perhaps not unique in kind, is probably *sui generis* in degree.

Aside from these considerations, however, there is no doubt that the theoretical views which Lenin had developed in *The State and Revolution* found reflection in his attitude toward the constitutional structure of the transitional dictatorship. Like the revolutionary state envisaged in his 1917 pamphlet, the Soviet state was set up to serve divergent and incompatible purposes. Anticipating a period of "unprecedentedly bitter class struggle," the temporary political authority which, in accordance with Lenin's analysis in *The State and Revolution*, would accomplish "the transition between the state and the no-state" (*perekhod ot gosudarstva k negosudarstvu*) had to be both "democratic *in a new way* (for the proletarians and the poor in general) and dictatorial *in a new way* (against the bourgeoisie)." [14]

Lenin's analysis of the fall of the Paris Commune, the acknowledged predecessor and model of the Soviet regime, culminated in the conclusion that it had not acted "decisively enough" in crushing the bourgeoisie. Accordingly, both before and after the Revolution Lenin stressed the repressive character, the negative nature and function, of the dictatorship of the proletariat. In *The State and Revolution*, he twice cited with approval the dictum by Engels that "the proletariat . . . needs the state . . . not in the interests of freedom, but in the interests of the repression of its opponents, and when it becomes possible to speak of freedom, the state as such ceases to exist." [15] As a matter of fact, following the example of Marx and Engels, Lenin regarded the state and freedom as a contradiction in terms. "As long as the state exists, there is no freedom. When there is freedom, there will be no state." [16]

On the other hand, Lenin emphasized the uniqueness, the novelty and democratic character of the proletarian state, describing it as the first dictatorship—and, indeed, government—in which the majority ruled over the minority. Manifesting a startling naïveté in regard to the practical problems of government and espousing ideas on economic organization and administration recalling the simplistic notions of Morelly, Buonarroti, and Saint-Simon, he called on the workers a few days after the October Revolution "to administer the state," to "take *all the affairs* of the state into *your own* hands." [17] Apparently, Lenin had no difficulty reconciling the idea of single-party dictatorship with the idea of direct mass democracy and saw no contradiction in principle between the more or less voluntary and decentralized association of the workers, implied in the concept of the withering away of the state, and the concentration of political power necessary to decisively crush the bourgeoisie.

Lenin's mental agility notwithstanding, there is no doubt that the Soviet state, from its very inception, suffered from what might be called ideological illegitimacy. Like Marx and Engels, Lenin had not been very precise in defining the nature and duration of the transition period. In *The State and Revolution*, Lenin had criticized the anarchists and had argued that the state could not be abolished "overnight," that the transition would require "a whole historical epoch." In the spring of 1918 he had estimated that the transition period would last "ten years or perhaps more," and a year later, in his May Day speech, he had predicted that "the majority of those present . . . who have not passed the age of 30–35 will see the golden age of communism, from which we are still far." [18] Nevertheless, he had committed himself to the proposition that "the proletarian state will begin to die away immediately after its victory, since in a society without class contradictions the state is unnecessary and impossible." [19] He had thought of the transition period in finite terms and expressed the conviction that the withering away of the state would be a continuous and progressive process beginning with the revolution. It was this prediction and commitment, together with the disillusionment produced by the dichotomy between revolutionary ideals and postrevolutionary practice in virtually all areas of life, which haunted Lenin's regime and called into question its legitimacy.

The socioeconomic and political dislocations and the terrible toll on the moral fabric of Russian society produced by the Civil War alone rendered any thought of an immediate transition to socialism an idle dream. Not counting the five "independent" governments set up under German occupation, e.g., the Ukraine and Lithuania, and the states which had formerly been a part of the Russian Empire but had now declared themselves independent, e.g., Georgia and Finland, at the height of that war no less than eighteen rival governments, scattered over the vast territory of Russia, challenged the authority of the Bolshevik regime in Moscow, which in the spring of 1918 became the capital of the Revolution—a move that ended the "Saint Petersburg era" in Russian history and was symbolic of the future orientalization and nationalist course of the Revolution. From 1918 to 1920 the "revolutionary" Reds and the "counterrevolutionary" Whites rivaled each other in atrocities. Roving bands of deserters, former prisoners of war, foreign interventionists, bandits and adventurers of various descriptions roamed the Russian countryside, terrorizing the population and contributing to the almost complete breakdown of all social cohesion and political authority. In the words of Boris Pasternak, it was a period which confirmed the ancient proverb "Man is a wolf to man." "Traveller turned off the road at the sight of traveller, stranger meeting stranger killed for fear of being killed. There were isolated cases of cannibalism. The laws of human civilization were suspended. The jungle law was in force. Man dreamed the prehistoric dreams of the cave dweller." [20] The Bolsheviks now reaped the harvest of the seeds of anarchism which they had so freely scattered before 1917. Almost from the very moment of the Bolshevik seizure of power in Petrograd, Lenin and his party were compelled by the force of circumstances to embark upon the most gigantic counterrevolution in the history of mankind.

The Civil War, the intervention of the foreign powers, the very dimensions of the socioeconomic transformation which the Bolsheviks sought to bring about, and, perhaps most important, the fact that the essential conditions for building the socialist order envisaged by Lenin had not yet developed in Russia—all were conducive to the aggrandizement of the state and militated against the early implementation of the kind of socialist order outlined in *The State and Revolution*. Addressing the Third All-Russian Congress of Soviets in January of 1918, Lenin still maintained that the present organization of Soviet power "clearly shows the transition towards the complete abolition of all power, of any state." [21] But when Bukharin proposed at the Seventh Party Congress in March 1918 that the revised party program should include a description of "the developed socialist order, i.e., communism," presumably an order in which there is no state, Lenin protested strongly, arguing that such a description would be premature and, in fact, impossible. "At the present time," he said, "we stand unconditionally for the state. . . ." He frankly admitted that "we cannot provide a characterization of socialism; we do not know what socialism will be like when it attains its final form . . ." For "the materials necessary for the characterization of socialism do not yet exist. The bricks out of which socialism will be built have not yet been fired . . ." In the meantime, his argument continued, the revolution needs the state. He predicted that there would be "time to convene more than two congresses before we can say: Look how our state is dying away. Until then it is too soon. To proclaim in advance the dying away of the state will be a violation of historical perspective." [22]

Thus, by March 1918, four months after the Bolshevik seizure of power, Lenin realized the futility of dreaming about the immediate realization of the socialist millennium, i.e., the creation of a classless and stateless society. The earlier confidence in the possibility of a quick and direct transition to socialism was gone. As a matter of fact, Lenin began to entertain doubts about whether the Bolsheviks would succeed in building a socialist order in Russia. The kinds of issues raised by Bukharin would become germane, he said, "*if* [*esli*] we arrive at socialism."

In July of 1919 Lenin delivered the first of two lectures on the state at Sverdlovsk University. He patiently explained the Marxist conception of the state as a coercive instrument, a "machine for the maintenance of the rule of one class over the others." In his concluding remarks, however, he admitted that in the right hands the state could serve positive and constructive purposes. And for this reason, the state would not be thrown on the scrap heap of history until all possibility of exploitation had been eliminated, until there were no longer any landowners and factory owners, or social conditions in which a few people lived in luxury and the others were starving.[23] The disappearance of the state, in other words, was relegated to the faraway future. In March 1920, finally, at a meeting of the Moscow Soviet celebrating the first anniversary of the founding of the Third International, Lenin in effect repudiated the theory of the withering away of the state. He told the assembled Communists that "it is impossible to approach the question of the state in the old way; in place of the old, bookish formulation of this question a new, practical formulation has developed as a result of the revolutionary movement." The advanced elements of the proletariat, he said, needed to close ranks, to "develop the old state and put it on a new basis." Reflecting on the first two and a half years of Soviet rule, he stated categorically: "To object to the necessity of a central power, a dictatorship and the unity of will . . . has become impossible after the experience we have gone through." [24] Although the idea of the ultimate withering away of the state under communism continued to occupy an important place in Soviet ideology and doctrine, the belief in the proximity of the stateless society became an early casualty of practical political experience. In the words of Louis Fischer, "life killed a beautiful theory."

Lenin's Political Legacy

Until the end of his life, Lenin continued to believe in the potential power of carefully planned and meticulously executed social engineering. He never lost his faith in the effectiveness of organization and reorganization. Even when death was already looking over his shoulder, he was preoccupied with organizational schemes designed to revamp the structure and functions of the top-level institutions of the government and the party. Throughout his life he retained his confidence in the ability of competent and dedicated men to shape the destiny of whole social classes and, indeed, an entire nation. To his credit, it must be said that in many ways Lenin learned from the political experience he gained as the head of the "Oblomov Republic," as he caustically described the Soviet state in moments of despair. His earlier faith in the effectiveness of governmental decrees slowly disintegrated in the face of the hard political lessons which life taught him after the Revolution. During 1921–22 we find in Lenin a growing realization of the enormous dimensions, the complexity, and the true magnitude of the task he had undertaken, as well as the recognition that there are limits to the ability and power of men to force the pace of history.

Even before the Kronstadt Rebellion in the winter of 1921—an anti-Bolshevik uprising of workers and sailors, supported by the majority of local Communists,

which aimed at returning the Revolution to the people
—Lenin had come to realize that his regime was rapidly
moving toward the edge of an abyss, that another
"breathing spell" was desperately needed, and that in
the long run a fundamental reorientation of policy was
necessary. It was this assessment which led to a series
of measures subsequently known as the New Economic
Policy or NEP, a policy which replaced the forced
requisitions under War Communism with a fixed tax in
kind and restored a measure of free enterprise—a policy,
in short, designed to serve as an antidote to the economic
chaos produced by War Communism. For once economics took precedence over politics. But there is little
doubt that for Lenin the catastrophic decline in industrial production, the virtual breakdown of state-controlled
distribution, the development of a runaway inflation,
the refusal of the peasant to deliver necessary grain sup-
plies to the towns, and the resulting population drain
from the industrial centers were all political problems of
the first order. At the Tenth Party Congress on March
15, 1921, he began the speech in which he formally submitted his proposals to the party by emphasizing that
"the question of replacing requisitions with a tax [in
kind] is first of all and above all a political question,
since the essence of this question involves the relationship of the working class to the peasantry"—a relationship which "determines the fate of our entire
revolution." [25]

As a student of von Clausewitz, Lenin knew when
to advance and when to retreat. Faced with the obsoles-
cence and failure of War Communism and aware of the
impracticability of socialism, he was willing to make
overtures to the peasant, to restore freedom of trade, to
return to a limited kind of capitalism. "What is needed,"

he told the delegates at the Tenth Party Congress, "is a much longer period of preparation, a slower tempo —that is the lesson life has taught us during this last year, a lesson which the party as a whole must especially and above all master, in order to determine our basic tasks during the coming year and in order to avoid . . . [similar] mistakes in the future." [26]

After twenty-one years of relentless struggle to force the pace of history, to "make the revolution now," to hurry the arrival of the "real day,"—i.e., the dawn of the new era which Dobroliubov had proclaimed in 1860— Lenin realized the futility of pursuing the goal of a rapid and direct transition to socialism in Russia. Thus, two and a half years after the October Revolution, at the age of fifty, he was finally prepared to shed this vestige of his Populist past.

In this tour de force of Bolshevik policy represented by the NEP, Lenin demonstrated some of the ingredients and qualities of great statesmanship. Unfortunately, his record was not uniform. The same year which saw the introduction of the NEP, the inauguration of the "Golden Age of Soviet rule," also brought the ruthless suppression of the revolt of the Kronstadt sailors (whom Trotsky at one time had called "the pride and glory of the Russian Revolution"), the virtual extinction of all organized political opposition to Bolshevism from independent parties,[27] and the consequential decree on party unity, which outlawed all factions within the party, thus destroying any hope for intraparty democracy and the democratic functioning of the Bolshevik Party within the context of a single-party state. The stage was now set for the fatal transformation of the Bolshevik Party into the political monolith and bureaucratic apparatus that, within a few years, would become the obedient instrument of Stalin. These measures to consolidate the Bolshevik dictatorship were followed, in the spring of 1922, by the transformation of the Cheka into the GPU—a transformation which resulted in the *de facto*, if not *de jure*, increase in the arbitrary power of the secret police, and, three months later, by the trial of the SR leaders, the first great political trial staged by the Soviet regime.

After the spring of 1921, during which Lenin himself for all practical purposes put an end to the legitimacy of any kind of intraparty opposition and masterminded the reorientation of the Soviet system along the lines of the NEP, "the dreamer in the Kremlin," as H. G. Wells characterized the Bolshevik leader, had one more year of active involvement in Soviet politics left. Like his father, who died at the age of fifty-four, Lenin was never to experience old age. In May 1922 he was to suffer a stroke. In the fall of that year he would return to work for a few weeks, only to be cut down by a second stroke in December which would make him an invalid until his death on January 21, 1924.

Lenin's declining health and prolonged illness compelled him to increasingly retire from the hustle and bustle of political life. By the force of circumstances, he had time to reflect—something all statesmen ought to have and few ever do. He was thus able to gain some distance and develop a perspective on his lifework.

There is evidence that Lenin, beginning in 1921, turned his attention more and more to the question of the quality of Soviet institutions as he became increasingly aware of the difficulties and obstacles which confronted him in his attempt to build a socialist society in Russia. "You can drive out the tsar . . . the landowners . . . [and] the capitalists," he wrote to M. F. Sokolov.

"This we have done. But you cannot 'drive out' bureaucratism in a peasant country, you cannot 'erase [it] from the face of the earth.' You can only reduce it through slow, persistent work. . . . In *this* case, surgery is absurd, *impossible*; only *slow healing* [can help], everything else is charlatanism or naïveté." [28] Had Lenin come to the realization that some sociopolitical problems do not admit of an easy and ready-made solution, no matter how well planned and how carefully executed?

The concern with bureaucracy became a dominant theme in Lenin's writings and correspondence during the closing years of his life. On January 24, 1922, he wrote to A. D. Tsiurupa, Deputy Chairman of the Council of People's Commissars, and complained about "the bureaucratic swamp" in which the whole Soviet system found itself. "Clever saboteurs are deliberately sucking us into this paper bog. . . . The center of gravity of your work must be precisely this transformation of our abominable bureaucratic work, the struggle against bureaucratism and red tape, the *check on the execution* [of instructions]." He included a list of things to do in order to "radically alter" the *modus operandi* of the top organs of the government, exhorting Tsiurupa to free himself "from the hustle and bustle which *is ruining all of us,* to give yourself the opportunity to think quietly about the *work as a whole.*" [29] Returning to the same subject a month later, he wrote to Tsiurupa that the most important thing now is "to study people, to find *capable* workers. Without this, all decrees and resolutions are dirty pieces of paper." Tsiurupa's prompt reply apparently did not please Lenin. "There is still a basic disagreement between us," he wrote the following day. "The main thing, in my opinion, is to move the center of gravity from the writing of decrees and decisions (in this we have been stupid to the point of idiocy) to the *selection of personnel* and the *verification of execution*. . . . Finding the right people and checking up on the work—that is everything." [30]

There is evidence that at the end of 1922 Lenin even began to question the principle of centralization, which had dominated his thinking concerning effective political organization ever since the turn of the century. Faced with the full complexity of the nationalities problem and with Stalin's "Great Russian-nationalistic campaign"—Lenin's own words!—in Georgia, he turned to decentralization as a possible solution. He developed his thoughts on the nationalities issue in a series of notes dictated at the end of December 1922. A nationalities policy based on injustice, he said, more than anything else, would retard "the development and consolidation of proletarian class solidarity." To grant the non-Russian nationalities mere formal equality would not be enough. What was needed was a complete reversal of the traditional nationalities policy pursued by czarist Russia. While the Union of Soviet Socialist Republics should be retained and strengthened in the realm of military and diplomatic affairs, and as a base for the worldwide proletarian struggle against capitalism, the constituent republics of the USSR should be given complete autonomy in all other affairs. In his last note on the nationalities problem, Lenin clearly envisaged the possibility of restricting the jurisdiction of the central government in Moscow exclusively to military and foreign affairs and granting "full independence of the separate people's commissariats [of the constituent republics] in all other respects." [31] Lenin did not deal with the difficult question of how the autonomy of the nationalities would be safeguarded against the encroachments of a centralized party apparatus. Nor did he wrestle with the problems raised by the kind of "limited sovereignty" which he proposed for the non-Russian nationalities. Nevertheless, he was apparently prepared to move rather far in the direction of decentralization and autonomy for the nationalities.

Decentralization, Lenin fully recognized, would not be an unmixed blessing, and cohesion would be needed to defend the Revolution against Western imperialism. But "the harm to our state which can result from the absence of unity between the [government] apparatuses of the nationalities and the Russian apparatus is immeasurably smaller, infinitely smaller, than the harm that can come not only to us, but to the whole International, to hundreds of millions among the peoples of Asia, which—following us—is about to make its debut on the historical scene in the very near future." It would be "unforgivable opportunism" if, precisely at the moment of their awakening and revolutionary debut, "we would undermine our authority" among the peoples of the East "through even the least rudeness and injustice in our relations with our own aliens [*inorodtsy*]." Even the hint of an imperialistic relationship toward the non-Russian nationalities, Lenin concluded, would completely undermine "our sincerity of principle, our whole defense of the struggle against imperialism." With the last flicker of the year 1922, Lenin, looking into the future, predicted that "the morrow of world history will be precisely such a day which will bring the awakening of the aroused peoples oppressed by imperialism and the beginning of the decisive, long and difficult struggle for their liberation." [32]

Writing in 1852, Alexander Herzen, the "Father of Russian Socialism" and the founder of Populism, still under the impression of the events of 1848 in Europe, had pointed to the East. "In the midst of this chaos, of these agonies of death and throes of birth," he had written in his famous essay on "The Russian People and Socialism," "in the midst of a world falling into dust at the foot of the cradle of the future, men's eyes involuntarily turn to the East." [33] Seventy years later, Lenin, the Marxist, followed Herzen's example. As the prospects of a revolution in Europe grew dimmer, Lenin increasingly turned his attention to the East and eventually transformed Bolshevism, which initially was a Western-oriented revolutionary doctrine, explicitly into an Eastern-oriented theory of world revolution—a theory which looked on the colonies as an anti-imperialist force and natural ally of the Russian proletariat. [34]

The theory of world revolution which Lenin developed toward the end of his life and bequeathed to subsequent generations was Eastern-oriented in two important and related respects. First of all, it viewed the process of world revolution as a long-drawn-out struggle taking place primarily in the awakening colonial East and not in the advanced countries of the West. As the much-hoped-for revolution in Europe failed to materialize, Lenin increasingly came to look on the backward and underdeveloped East as the new storm center of the world revolution. Second, Lenin's theory of world revolution telescoped the Marxian idea of class struggle into a life and death conflict between East and West. Thus, the idea of *Klassenkampf*—itself the projection of Marx's concept of alienated man, of man as a dual self at war with himself, i.e., an idea which began as an attempt to explain the psychology of individual man [35]— through the mediation of Lenin was transformed into a theory of world revolution which assumed the character and dimensions of a theory of international relations. In his last published article, Lenin explained that this struggle was between "the counter-revolutionary imperialist West and the revolutionary and nationalist East, between the most civilized countries of the world and the orientally [*po-vostochnomu*] backward countries." [36] In short, toward the end of his life Lenin had come to the conclusion that the future struggle between capitalism and communism would basically be an East-West conflict. Thus we find him writing in 1923:

. . . As the result of the last imperialist war, a number of countries—the East, China, India, etc.—have been completely dislodged from their groove. Their development has definitely turned toward the general European capitalist model. They have begun to experience the general European ferment, and it is now clear to the whole world that they have been drawn into a process of development that cannot but lead to a crisis in the whole of world capitalism.

. . . Precisely because of this first imperialist war, the East has definitely been drawn into the revolutionary movement . . . into the general maelstrom of the world revolutionary movement.

. . . In the final analysis, the outcome of the struggle will be determined by the fact that Russia, India, China, etc., constitute the overwhelming majority of the population [of the globe]. And it is precisely this majority which, in the course of the last few years, has been drawn into the struggle for its liberation with extraordinary rapidity, so that in this respect there cannot be a shadow of a doubt about what the final outcome of the world struggle will be. In this sense, the ultimate victory of socialism is completely and unconditionally assured. [37]

But while Lenin expressed his unreserved confidence in the ultimate success of the world revolution, he was much less sanguine about the future of the political regime he had created. As a matter of fact, there is a note of despair and resignation in most of his last writings concerning various Soviet institutions. In a series of articles which, according to Bukharin, formed only a part of the political testament Lenin had intended to leave behind,[38] the tired revolutionary, already weakened and partially incapacitated by a series of strokes, frankly admitted that "we have been compelled to acknowledge a radical change in our entire point of view concerning socialism" and clearly expressed his dissatisfaction with the quality of existing Soviet institutions. The former preoccupation with political struggle and revolution had to be replaced by a new emphasis on "peaceful, organizational 'cultural' work." In fact, what was needed was a "whole period of cultural development," a "cultural revolution" which would require a "whole epoch" and bring universal literacy, efficiency, and the necessary material basis for socialism to Russia. "For a start," Lenin wrote in a mood of resignation, "we would be satisfied with real bourgeois culture." [39]

As far as governmental institutions were concerned, Lenin said in so many words, the situation was "deplorable, not to say disgusting." With the exception of the People's Commissariat for Foreign Affairs, the Soviet state was essentially "a typical relic of the old state machine." After five years of "haste" and "bustle," which have "clogged up our institutions and our brains . . . we must come to our senses in time." [40] Lenin's last article, "Better Fewer, But Better," was an eloquent plea to decrease the pace, to go slow, to rebuild the entire machinery of the state and reduce it to the bare minimum, to strive for "really exemplary quality" in government, to "measure your cloth seven times before you cut," to involve the working class in the process of government in a meaningful way.

One of the last significant acts of Lenin as party leader and Chairman of the powerful *Sovnarkom*, i.e., the Council of People's Commissars, was an attempt to separate the party from the government. However, in spite of unanimity on this question at the Eleventh Party Congress in 1922, the division of functions conceived by Lenin never came about. When S. V. Kossior, a trade union leader, complained about the constant interference of the Politburo, i.e., the top leadership body in the party, even in such minor matters as the appointment of third-rank officials, Lenin came down on the side of the party, arguing that "the Politburo of the Central Committee has in its time made a minimum of mistakes." The right to appoint key bureaucrats and minor officials in the government, as well as in the mass organizations affiliated with the party, remained the exclusive prerogative of the Politburo. As subsequent events were to show, this prerogative, along with others, not only rendered the separation between party and government desired by Lenin meaningless in practice, but also significantly contributed to the political rise of Stalin. Within a few years, the party swallowed the government, and then, after Stalin mounted his attack on the Bolshevik Party in the purges of the 1930s, the party itself was eclipsed by the personal government of Russia's new autocrat.

While the phenomenon of Stalinism itself cannot be separated from the personality and psychology of Joseph Dzhugashvili-Stalin or "Koba," the "wonderful Georgian" whom Lenin co-opted to the Central Committee in 1912, there is little doubt that the essential conditions for its emergence were, to a large extent, created by Lenin himself. In the consequential decree on party unity passed at the Tenth Party Congress in 1921, he gave Stalin an ideal instrument for dealing with intraparty opposition. In his essay on the "History of the Question of Dictatorship," written in 1920, Lenin himself provided an accurate description and ideological justification of the kind of political order which Stalin set up a few years later. "The scientific concept of dictatorship," he wrote, "means nothing other than unlimited government, unrestrained by any laws [or] absolute rules, supporting itself directly by the use of force." [41] Perhaps most important, Lenin explicitly endorsed the use of mass terror after the October Revolution; he declared categorically in January 1918 that "we can achieve nothing unless we use terror," sharply criticized the Petrograd party leaders in June for restraining the "revolutionary initiative of the masses" in their desire to unleash a campaign of indiscriminate terror against the former middle class, and exhorted the Nizhni Novgorod Soviet in August to "apply mass terror immediately, to execute and exterminate hundreds of prostitutes, drunken soldiers, former officers, etc." On May 17, 1922, Lenin wrote a letter to D. I. Kursky, Commissar of Justice, about the proposed new criminal code and recommended the inclusion of an additional paragraph which would openly proclaim the necessity, justification, and legitimacy of terror.

Stalin, however, was not only indebted to Lenin for some of the essential conditions and instruments which made the *Stalinshchina*, i.e., the Time of Stalin, possible; he also owed to him his position as General Party Secretary. Stalin had made his mark in Soviet government as Commissar of Nationalities and as head of *Rabkrin*, i.e., the special Commissariat of Workers' and Peasants' Inspection charged with watching the activities of the other ministries and combating bureaucracy. But it was as General Secretary of the Russian Communist Party—a position created in 1922 as a temporary expedient during Lenin's illness—that Stalin, after April 1922, began his rapid political ascent.

There is some evidence that it was Kamenev, not Lenin, who proposed the creation of the office of General Secretary and nominated Stalin for the new post—a post which in 1922 was not regarded as particularly important. Stalinist claims notwithstanding, the election of Stalin as General Secretary did not signify that he had been designated as Lenin's successor. Quite possibly, Stalin's election was presented to Lenin as a *fait accompli*. In any case, Lenin apparently acquiesced to the Central Committee's choice of Stalin.[42]

Lenin subsequently tried to curb Stalin's "boundless power" by proposing an enlarged Central Committee and increased prerogatives for the State Planning Commission (*Gosplan*), and generally reducing the functions of the central government. Aware of Stalin's "rudeness" and "disposition toward fiat administration," Lenin, in a postscript to his secret testament, written on January 4, 1923, proposed to demote Stalin and intended to "crush [him] politically"—as Krupskaya told Kamenev on March 6 of that year. But Lenin never had a chance to carry out his intentions. On March 7, 1923, he suffered another serious attack which paralyzed half his body and deprived him of his ability to speak. Although still alive physically, the Bolshevik leader was politically finished.

The last thoughts and actions of the greatest revolutionary of all time provide a startling contrast to what the future held in store for the Russian people. In 1923, on the eve of Lenin's death, the Soviet Union was far from the attainment of the ideals which had motivated the Revolution. As the dying Lenin, fully aware that his former comrades had already begun to bury him,[43] cast a parting glance over the Russia he was leaving behind, he must have realized the extent to which he had failed in his attempt to give wings to reality. Indeed, in many respects his efforts had turned into the very opposite of what he had originally intended. And thus Lenin, in a retrospective evaluation of his lifework, might have said with Dostoevsky's Shigalev: "I am confused by my own findings: my conclusion is a direct contradiction of the original idea from which I start. Taking as my point of departure the idea of unlimited freedom, I arrive at unlimited despotism." [44]

NOTES

◫ ◫ ◫

AUTHOR'S PREFACE

1. *Lenina chitaet ves' mir* (Moscow: Izdatel'stvo "Kniga," 1970), pp. 13, 23.

2. Léon Trotsky, *Vie de Lénine. Jeunesse.* Traduction de Maurice-Parijanine. (Paris: Les Éditions Rieder, 1936). A German translation appeared as Leo Trotzki, *Der junge Lenin.* Nach dem russischen Originalmanuskript ins Deutsche übertragen von Walter Fischer. (Vienna: Verlag Fritz Molden, 1969). This important study has recently been published as Leon Trotsky, *The Young Lenin.* Translation and Introduction by Max Eastman. (Garden City: Doubleday & Company, 1972).

3. Richard Pipes, "The Origins of Bolshevism: The Intellectual Evolution of Young Lenin," in *Revolutionary Russia,* ed. R. Pipes (Cambridge: Harvard University Press, 1969), pp. 26–62.

4. Isaac Deutscher, *Lenin's Childhood* (London: Oxford University Press, 1970).

5. Nikolai Valentinov, *The Early Years of Lenin.* Trans. and ed. Rolf H. W. Theen. Foreword by Bertram D. Wolfe. (Ann Arbor: University of Michigan Press, 1969).

CHAPTER 1

1. For information on Lenin's pseudonyms, see I. N. Vol'per, *Psevdonimy V. I. Lenina* ([Leningrad]: Lenizdat, 1965), especially pp. 38 ff.

2. Circumstantial evidence suggests that Lenin's paternal grandfather was a Tatar or a Kalmyk. His name and membership in the Greek Orthodox Church, on the other hand,

suggest that he may have been a Great Russian. See Marietta Shaginian, "Predki Lenina," *Novyi mir,* no. 11 (November 1937), pp. 269–70; Georg von Rauch, "Lenins Vorfahren im Lichte der Biographien," *Osteuropa,* vol. XX, no. 4 (April 1970), pp. 225–26; and Isaac Deutscher, *op. cit.,* pp. 2–4.

3. Deutscher (*op. cit.,* p. 2), apparently following Shaginian (*op. cit.,* p. 267), incorrectly implies that Lenin's father was born in 1832 or 1833. The correct date of birth is July 14 (26), 1831. See A. I. Ivanskii, ed., *Molodye gody V. I. Lenina. Po vospominaniiam i dokumentam* (Moscow: Izdatel'stvo TsK VLKSM "Molodaia gvardiia," 1957), p. 7, and Shaginian, *op. cit.,* p. 280. In the 1830s, Astrakhan municipal records referred to Lenin's grandfather as Ulyanov, Ulyaninov, and Ulyanin, i.e., three different but similar-sounding names. (See *ibid.,* p. 271, and Ivanskii, *op. cit.,* p. 7.) Assuming the absence of clerical errors, this fact suggests that he had only recently acquired a family name when he left the ranks of the serfs, who were commonly known only by their Christian names and patronymics.

4. The term *"meshchanin"* is difficult to translate. It refers to lower-middle-class town dwellers. Although they were free by comparison with the serfs, they had no political rights, were subject to corporal punishment, did not enjoy unrestricted freedom of movement, and could be admitted to the civil service only by special dispensation of the czar or one of his ministers.

5. More specifically, Lenin's father was excluded from the civil service because he belonged to an estate which was subject to taxation (*podatnoe sostoianie*). This and subsequent information about Lenin's father is based on Ivanskii, *op. cit.,* pp. 8 ff., and Shaginian, *op. cit.,* pp. 280 ff.

6. Ivanskii, *op. cit.,* p. 12.

7. The possibility of Lenin's Jewish ancestry has always intrigued his political opponents and critics. According to N. Valentinov ("O predkakh Lenina i ego biografiiakh," *Novyi zhurnal,* no. 61 [1960], p. 222), there were attempts among the *chernosotentsy,* i.e., the extreme rightist circles of 1905–7, to prove that Lenin was a Jew. In the 1920s and 1930s, Hitler and his followers seized on Lenin's alleged

Jewish ancestry as evidence of the existence of a "Jewish-Bolshevik conspiracy." Even some high-ranking Communists have raised this same issue. Thus, for example, Trotsky remarked about the reticence of Soviet writers to deal with the question of Lenin's maternal ancestry; and Karl Radek, who—like Trotsky—was himself a Jew, intimated in an article on Lenin's parents ("Roditeli," *Izvestiia*, April 23, 1933, p. 2) that Lenin may have had Jewish ancestors. More recently, this question has been the subject of a heated controversy in the Russian émigré press, notably between N. Valentinov, A. Burgina, and D. Shub, who quotes Lenin as having said that "the clever Russian [*russkii umnik*] is almost always a Jew or an individual with an admixture of Jewish blood." (See David Shub, "Po povodu stat'i N. Valentinova i pis'ma v redaktsiiu 'Istorika,'" *Novyi zhurnal*, no. 63 [1961], p. 290. Shub cites from M. Gorkii, *Vladimir Lenin* [Leningrad, 1924], p. 20. In later editions of this work, this remark was expurgated.) In spite of the extensive literature on the subject, there is no conclusive evidence that Lenin's maternal grandfather was a Jew. On the other hand, the possibility of a Jewish element in Lenin's ancestry cannot be excluded. If one approaches this issue without prejudice, the question of Lenin's ancestry becomes important only because of the demand for exactitude in research.

8. Cf. Georg von Rauch, "Lenins Lübecker Ahnen," *Zeitschrift des Vereins für Lübeckische Geschichte und Altertumskunde*, vol. 40 (1960), pp. 98–101; Ivanskii, *op. cit.*, pp. 11 ff.; and *Vospominaniia o Vladimire Il'iche Lenine* (Moscow: Gosudarstvennoe izdatel'stvo politicheskoi literatury, 1956) [hereafter cited as *Vosp.* (1956)], Vol. I, pp. 12 ff. According to some sources, Dr. Blank also had a son, Dimitri, who lived on the estate at Kokushkino. (See S. T. Possony, *Lenin: The Compulsive Revolutionary* [Chicago: Henry Regnery Company, 1964], p. 4). The Kokushkino household may also have included a great-aunt, Karoline Öhrstedt. (See von Rauch, "Lenins Vorfahren im Lichte der Biographien," p. 230.)

9. Louis Fischer, *The Life of Lenin* (New York: Harper & Row, 1964), pp. 1, 4.

10. Nikolai Valentinov, *The Early Years of Lenin*, p.

43. M. Shaginian reported her findings on Lenin's paternal ancestry in 1937 in the above-cited article in *Novyi mir*, together with facsimile documents. A remark in that article (p. 271) suggests that she may have intended to publish a second essay dealing with Lenin's maternal ancestry. Her novel, *Bilet po istorii. Sem'ia Ul'ianovykh*, was first published in *Krasnaia nov'*, no. 5 (1937), and appeared as a book in 1938. Although reportedly well received by both Krupskaya, Lenin's wife, and Dimitri Ulyanov, Lenin's brother, the novel met with the disapproval of the party authorities and resulted in a Politburo order, dated August 5, 1938, banning the publication of memoirs and scholarly and artistic books about Lenin. This ban was lifted by a Central Committee decree of October 11, 1956. (See *Spravochnik partiinogo rabotnika* [Moscow: Gosudarstvennoe izdatel'stvo politicheskoi literatury, 1957], [vypusk 1], p. 364.) An expanded version of Shaginian's 1937 essay was published in *Astrakhan. Literaturno-khudozhestvennyi sbornik* (1958). A revised and expanded version of the novel appeared in the journal *Neva*, no. 8 (1957), pp. 3–69, and as a book, with a most interesting and revealing note from the publisher, in 1958. (Cf. M. S. Shaginian, *Sem'ia Ul'ianovykh* [Moscow: Izdatel'stvo TsK VLKSM "Molodaia gvardiia," 1958]. See also Marietta Shaginian, *Sem'ia Ul'ianovykh. Ocherki. Stat'i. Vospominaniia* [Moscow: Gosudarstvennoe izdatel'stvo khudozhestvennoi literatury, 1959], pp. 5–133.) The post-Stalin version of the novel has also been published in German translation as Marietta Schaginjan, *Die Familie Uljanow* (Berlin: Verlag Kultur und Fortschritt, 1959). In 1972 Shaginian received the Lenin Prize for her books on the Ulyanov family. (See *Pravda*, April 22, 1972, p. 3.)

11. See the latest "scientific" biography by P. N. Pospelov *et al.*, eds. *Vladimir Il'ich Lenin. Biografiia* (Moscow: Gosudarstvennoe izdatel'stvo politicheskoi literatury, 1960), pp. 1, 2, and later editions, where the reader is told that Lenin's father came from "a lower middle-class family" and that Lenin's mother was "the daughter of a physician."

12. According to Fischer (*op. cit.*, p. 6), a boy, Nikolai, was born in 1873 and died in the same year. Possony (*op.*

cit., pp. [xvii], 6) reports another daughter, Olga, who was born and died in 1868. As far as I know, there is no reference to these children in the memoirs of the Ulyanov family or in Soviet sources on Lenin. They are not mentioned in Bertram D. Wolfe, *Three Who Made a Revolution* (Boston: Beacon Press, 1962), pp. 39 ff., and Adam B. Ulam, *The Bolsheviks* (New York: The Macmillan Company, 1965), p. 6.

13. Ivanskii, *op. cit.*, pp. 21–22.

14. Valentinov, *The Early Years of Lenin*, p. 91.

15. When Ilya Nikolaevich died in 1886, there were 434 primary schools with a combined enrollment of about 20,000 pupils and several excellent secondary schools in Simbirsk *guberniia*—a remarkable achievement considering that there had been only 20 schools in operation in 1870.

16. Actual Councilor of State was the fourth highest civilian rank in a table of fourteen ranks. It corresponded to the military rank of major general. People were obliged to address holders of this rank as "Vashe Prevoskhoditel'stvo," i.e., "Your Excellency."

17. This characterization of Lenin's mother is largely based on the memoirs of her oldest daughter. See A. I. Ul'ianova-Elizarova, *Vospominaniia ob Il'iche* ([Moscow]: Molodaia gvardiia, 1935), pp. 12–13.

18. N. K. Krupskaya, "Childhood and Early Years of Ilyich," in *Reminiscences of Lenin by His Relatives* (Moscow: Foreign Languages Publishing House, 1956), p. 194.

19. Cf. G. A. Solomon, *Lenin i ego sem'ia* (Ul'ianovy) (Paris: Imprimerie des Travailleurs Intellectuels, 1931), p. 26. See also Lenin's *Letters to Relatives, 1893–1922*, including more than 150 letters to his mother, in V. I. Lenin, *Polnoe sobranie sochinenii* (Moscow: Gosudarstvennoe izdatel'stvo politicheskoi literatury, 1960–65), 5th ed. [hereafter cited as *PSS*], vol. 55.

20. See *Perepiska sem'i Ul'ianovykh, 1883–1917* (Moscow: Izdatel'stvo politicheskoi literatury, 1969).

21. Shaginian, "Predki Lenina," p. 264. Occasionally Maria Aleksandrovna was described as Greek Orthodox in official documents, e.g., the registry of Lenin's birth. (Cf.

Ivanskii, *op. cit.*, p. 46.) However, there is no evidence that she ever accepted the Greek Orthodox faith, even formally.

22. Shaginian, "Predki Lenina," p. 264.

23. See Lenin's reply to a party questionnaire, dated February 13, 1922, in Lenin, *PSS*, vol. 44, p. 509.

24. Krupskaya reports that "the fact that his sons had abandoned religion caused him [i.e., Ilya Nikolaevich] anxiety." (Krupskaya, *op. cit.*, p. 192.) However, only Sasha abandoned religion during his father's lifetime.

25. The prolonged absence of a parent in early childhood tends to create feelings of neglect, insecurity, and mistrust. See Otto Fenichel, *The Psychoanalytical Theory of Neurosis* (New York: Norton, 1945), p. 44.

26. E. Victor Wolfenstein, *The Revolutionary Personality: Lenin, Trotsky, Gandhi* (Princeton: Princeton University Press, 1967), pp. 38–40, 97 ff. Wolfenstein's approach is intriguing. However, the absence of autobiographical, diary, or other reliable information about Lenin's childhood and adolescence imposes severe limitations.

27. Valentinov, *The Early Years of Lenin*, p. 26.

28. Ul'ianova-Elizarova, *op. cit.*, p. 14. All the Ulyanov children eventually became Marxists, Social-Democrats, and —following Lenin—Bolsheviks. All of them were subjected to imprisonment and exile at various times in Astrakhan, Nizhni Novgorod, and Vologda. The fact that all of them repeatedly traveled abroad suggests that the czarist secret police did not always impede their freedom of movement and that the Ulyanov family was more affluent than Soviet biographers would have us believe.

After the Revolution, Anna worked in the People's Commissariat for Education (*Narkompros*) from 1918 to 1921. In 1921 she joined *Istpart*, a commission of the Central Committee of the Russian Communist Party and of the Communist Party of the Soviet Union for the study of party history and the history of the Revolution. She edited the journal *Tkach* [*Weaver*] and became the secretary of the journal *Proletarskaia revoliutsiia*, as well as a member of the Central Committee. From 1928 to 1932 she worked in the Marx-Engels-Lenin Institute. Her husband, M. T. Elizarov

(1862–1919), was for a short time People's Commissar for Communication.

Dimitri Ulyanov studied medicine at Moscow University and in 1919 became Deputy Chairman of the Council of People's Commissars of the short-lived Crimean Republic. After 1921 he held an important post in the People's Commissariat for Public Health.

Maria Ulyanova became a secretary and later a member of the editorial board of *Pravda*. In 1925 she was elected to the Central Control Commission and in 1934 to the Commission of Soviet Control. In 1935 she became a member of the Central Executive Committee of the USSR.

29. Valentinov, *The Early Years of Lenin*, p. 26.

30. When Soviet troops entered Western Europe in 1945, they were generally thought to consist exclusively of "Mongols, Tatars, or Kalmyks." But they were Russian troops.

31. *Ibid.*, p. 17.

32. Ivanskii, *op. cit.*, p. 112.

33. *Ibid.*, pp. 187–89, 257.

34. *Ibid.*, p. 194.

35. A. Elizarova, "Vospominaniia ob Aleksandre Il'iche Ul'ianove," *Proletarskaia revoliutsiia*, no. 2–3 (1927), p. 287.

36. Valentinov, *The Early Years of Lenin*, pp. 61 ff.

37. In 1893 Lenin told Lalaiants: "For me, as well as for the whole family, the participation of my brother in the March 1 affair came as a complete surprise." See I. Lalaiants, "O moikh vstrechakh s V. I. Leninym za vremia 1893–1900 gg.," *Proletarskaia revoliutsiia*, no. 1 (84), (1929), p. 49.

38. Wolfenstein (*op. cit.*, pp. 97–98) has argued that the death of his father caused in Lenin "the adolescent reactivation of the Oedipal struggle" and the execution of Sasha "a double burden of guilt." "Psychologically speaking," he writes, "the two [deaths] in combination created a mighty impulse towards revolution."

39. Ivanskii, *op. cit.*, p. 184. Cf. also A. S. Poliakov, *Vtoroe l-e marta* (Moscow, 1919) and A. I. Ul'ianova-Elizarova, comp., *Aleksandr Il'ich Ul'ianov i delo l marta*

1887 g. Sbornik (Moscow-Leningrad: Gosudarstvennoe izdatel'stvo, 1927).

40. Ivanskii, *op. cit.,* p. 193.

41. *Ibid.,* p. 186.

42. *Ibid.,* p. 185.

43. "Nachalo puti. Avtobiograficheskie vyskazyvaniia V. I. Lenina (1886–1893)," *Novyi mir,* Vol. XXXIX, no. 4 (April 1963), p. 163.

44. A. Ul'ianova-Elizarova, "Lenin," *Deiateli Soiuza Sovetskikh Sotsialisticheskikh Respublik i Oktiabr'skoi Revoliutsii* (Moscow: Entsiklopedicheskii slovar' Russkogo bibliograficheskogo instituta Granat, 1929) [henceforth cited as *Deiateli*], p. 306.

45. Lenin, *PSS,* vol. 32, p. 21.

46. In the most complete edition of Lenin's works and correspondence published to date, Alexander Ulyanov is mentioned, incidentally, only one other time. (See *ibid.,* vol. 54, p. 14.)

CHAPTER 2

1. For a partial list of materials that have not been published—at least not *in toto*—see A. Ivanskii, comp., *Molodoi Lenin: Povest' v dokumentakh i memuarakh* (Moscow: Izdatel'stvo politicheskoi literatury, 1964), pp. 748–59. The difficulties of the biographer are compounded by the absence of any significant writings by Lenin prior to the spring of 1893. The most complete bibliography of Lenin's works lists only marginal items—petitions, telegrams, and certificates—for the first twenty-three years of his life. See *Khronologicheskii ukazatel' proizvedenii V. I. Lenina* (Moscow: Gosudarstvennoe izdatel'stvo politicheskoi literatury, 1959–62), Vol. I, pp. 1–9; Vol. II, p. 647.

2. *Pravda,* February 8, 1924, p. 3. Cf. also *Vladimir Il'ich* Lenin. *Biograficheskaia khronika* (Moscow: Izdatel'stvo politicheskoi literatury, 1970) [hereafter cited as *Biograf. khronika*], Vol. I (1870–1905), p. 25.

3. A. Elizarova, "Vospominaniia ob Aleksandre Il'iche Ul'ianove," p. 287, and Valentinov, *The Early Years of*

Lenin, p. 68. According to some sources, Lenin began reading Marx in the fall or winter of 1888. See A. I. Ul'ianova-Elizarova, "Vospominaniia ob Il'iche," in V*osp*. (1956), p. 21, and I. I. Bliumental', V. *I. Lenin v Samare* (Samara: Gubizdat, 1925), p. 6.

4. Ivanskii, ed., *Molodye gody V. I. Lenina*, p. 173.

5. *Ibid.*, p. 184; P. P. Elizarov, *Mark Elizarov i sem'ia Ul'ianovykh* (Moscow: Izdatel'stvo politicheskoi literatury, 1967), p. 16; and Solomon, *op. cit.*, pp. 24–25.

6. Ivanskii, *Molodoi Lenin*, p. 321.

7. According to some sources, Lenin was barred from the capital universities, i.e., Moscow and Saint Petersburg. (*Ibid.*) However, two years later his sister Olga pursued a course of higher studies in Saint Petersburg, and his brother Dimitri studied medicine at Moscow University in the 1890s. According to other sources, Lenin's mother was told by the local director of police that it would be better if her son enrolled in one of the provincial universities, preferably Kazan University. See B. Volin, *Lenin v Povolzh'e, 1870–1893* (Moscow: Gosudarstvennoe izdatel'stvo politicheskoi literatury, 1956), p. 44.

8. *Biograf. khronika*, Vol. I, pp. 30–31.

9. *Ibid.*, pp. 30–33, and Ivanskii, *Molodoi Lenin*, pp. 344–98.

10. Lenin, *PSS*, Vol. 1, p. 551.

11. G. E. Khait, "V Kazanskom kruzhke," *Novyi mir*, no. 4 (1958), pp. 190–92; M. K. Korbut, "Kazanskoe revoliutsionnoe podpol'e kontsa 80-kh godov i Lenin," *Katorga i ssylka*, no. 8/9 (81/82), (1931), pp. 7–27; *Krasnyi arkhiv*, no. 62 (1934), p. 65. For information on Bogoraz, cf. *Deiateli revoliutsionnogo dvizheniia v Rossii. Bio-bibliograficheskii slovar'* (Moscow: Vsesoiuznoe obshchestvo politicheskikh katorzhan i ssyl'no-poselentsev, 1931), Vol. V, vyp. 1, p. 398.

12. V. Adoratskii, "Za 18 let (Vstrechi s Vladimirom Il'ichem)," *Proletarskaia revoliutsiia*, no. 3 (26), (1924), p. 94; Ivanski, comp., *Molodoi Lenin*, pp. 402–3.

13. Valentinov, *op. cit.*, p. 194.

14. Lenin, *PSS* vol. 24, p. 294.

15. Valentinov, *op. cit.*, pp. 135–36. (Emphasis added in the sentence beginning "But then. . . ." The transliteration

of Chernyshevsky's name has been changed in the interest of conformity.) Chernyshevsky himself seems to have had doubts concerning the literary merit of *What Is to Be Done?* In the introductory part of his novel he addressed himself to his readers and dealt with the imaginary charge of "lack of artistic talent." Cf. N. G. Chernyshevskii, *Chto delat'?* (Moscow-Leningrad: Academia, 1937), p. 13.

16. Lenin, *PSS*, vol. 18, p. 384. The crucial influence of Chernyshevsky on Lenin was confirmed by the publication of Lenin's marginal notes on Steklov's biography of the famous editor of *Sovremennik*. See "Pometki V. I. Lenina na knige Iu. M. Steklova 'N. G. Chernyshevskii, ego zhizn' i deiatel'nost' (1909),'" *Literaturnoe nasledstvo*, Vol. LXVII (1959), pp. 9–78, and Lenin, *PSS*, vol. 29, pp. 572–620.

17. Valentinov, *op. cit.*, pp. 189 ff., and, by the same author, "Chernyshevskii i Lenin," *Novyi zhurnal*, no. 26 (1951), pp. 193–216, and no. 27 (1951), pp. 225–49.

18. Valentinov, *The Early Years of Lenin*, pp. 195–96; see also *Voprosy literatury*, no. 8 (1957), pp. 133–34.

19. M. Essen, "Vstrechi s Leninym," in *Vosp.* (1956), p. 292, and Ivanskii, *Molodoi Lenin*, p. 423.

20. G. V. Plekhanov, *Sochineniia* (Moscow: Gosudarstvennoe izdatel'stvo, n.d.), Vol. V, pp. 114–15.

21. Cf. the petition of M. A. Ulyanova to the Minister of Public Education, dated May 17, 1890, in *Krasnaia letopis'*, no. 2 (1924), p. 35; see also Ivanskii, *Molodye gody V. I. Lenina*, p. 303.

22. For information on Lenin's "legal career," cf. I. B. Sternik, *V. I. Lenin—Iurist* (Tashkent: Izdatel'stvo "Uzbekistan," 1969) and V. Shalaginov, *Zashchita poruchena Ul'ianovu* ([Novosibirsk]: Zapadno-Sibirskoe knizhnoe izdatel'stvo, 1967).

23. N. Valentinov, "Vstrecha Lenina s marksizmom," *Novyi zhurnal*, no. 53 (1958), pp. 189–208.

24. *Biograf. khronika*, Vol. I, p. 55.

25. Cf. *Novyi mir*, no. 4 (1957), p. 147; *Moskva*, no. 4 (1958), p. 55; and Valentinov, *The Early Years of Lenin*, pp. 141 ff. According to one source, Lenin was in direct contact with Sabunaev in December of 1889. See S. S. Volk,

Narodnaia Volia, 1879–1882 (Moscow-Leningrad: Izdatel'-stvo "Nauka," 1966), p. 448.

26. N. Valentinov, *Vstrechi s Leninym* (New York: Izdatel'stvo imeni Chekhova, 1953), p. 39.

27. Dolgov had been a member of *Narodnaia Rasprava*, Nechaev's organization, and a participant in the Dolgushin conspiracy organized by the followers of Nechaev. In Samara Lenin also became acquainted with another member of the Dolgushin group, A. I. Livanov. (Cf. Ivanskii, *Molodoi Lenin*, p. 627.) On Dolgov, cf. *Deiateli revoliutsionnogo dvizheniia v Rossii. Bio-bibliograficheskii slovar'* (Moscow: Vsesoiuznoe obshchestvo politicheskikh katorzhan i ssyl'no-poselentsev, 1928), Vol. I, pt. 2, p. 106.

28. M. Golubeva, "Poslednii karaul," *Molodaia gvardiia,* no. 2–3 (1924), p. 30, and, by the same author, "Moia pervaia vstrecha s Vladimirom Il'ichem," in *Vosp.* (1956), p. 113. As in the case of Chetvergova, Lenin would not forget these early associations. He corresponded with Golubeva in 1904. See *PSS*, vol. 46, pp. 387–88, 427.

29. Ivanskii, *Molodoi Lenin,* p. 530.

30. See, for example, Volin, *op. cit.,* pp. 73 ff., and Korbut, *op. cit.,* p. 24.

31. Lenin, *PSS*, vol. 45, p. 324.

32. An excerpt from the unpublished memoirs of Mandel'shtam suggests that before 1928 he did not know Lenin had been present at one of his lectures in Kazan. See *Moskva,* no. 4 (1958), p. 57.

33. See her memoirs in *Vosp.* (1956), p. 25.

34. Lenin, *PSS*, vol. 6, pp. 180–81.

35. A. Ul'ianova-Elizarova, "Lenin," in *Deiateli,* p. 309.

36. N. A. Alekseev, "V. I. Lenin v Londone (1902–1903 gg.)," in *Vosp.* (1956), p. 250.

37. Lenin, *PSS*, vol. 43, p. 417.

38. Although during the years 1904–5 Lenin defended "Jacobinism" and described the Bolsheviks as "the Jacobins of contemporary Social Democracy," he became increasingly sensitive to the charges of his political opponents and subsequently tried to dissociate Bolshevism and Jacobinism, at least in his public position. (Cf. *ibid.,* vol. 8, p. 370, and

vol. 11, p. 47.) For an interesting insight into Lenin's "private" views on the subject of Jacobinism, see Valentinov, *Vstrechi s Leninym*, pp. 185 ff.

CHAPTER 3

1. Bertram D. Wolfe, *An Ideology in Power: Reflections on the Russian Revolution* (New York: Stein and Day, 1969), pp. 164, 180.

2. Leonard Schapiro, "Lenin After Fifty Years," in L. Schapiro and P. Reddaway, eds., *Lenin: The Man, the Theorist, the Leader* (New York: Frederick A. Praeger, 1968), p. 19.

3. Boris Pasternak, *Dr. Zhivago* (New York: Pantheon, 1958), p. 461.

4. Leon Trotsky, who in his famous *History of the Russian Revolution* had tried to demonstrate the historical inevitability of the October Revolution and its roots in the objective socioeconomic conditions of Old Russia, concluded in private in 1935 that there would have been no October Revolution without Lenin. See *Trotsky's Diary in Exile, 1935*. Transl. by Elena Zarudnaya (Cambridge: Harvard University Press, 1958), p. 46.

5. R. N. Carew Hunt, *The Theory and Practice of Communism* (Baltimore: Penguin Books, 1964), p. 159. At least one Western scholar has argued that a knowledge of nineteenth-century Russian social thought is not necessary for an understanding of Leninism. See A. Meyer, *Leninism* (Cambridge: Harvard University Press, 1957), p. 7.

6. On this point, see the thoughtful essay by Peter Scheibert, "Über Lenins Anfänge," *Historische Zeitschrift*, no. 182 (1956), pp. 549–66.

7. Cf. V. I. Semevskii, *Politicheskie i obshchestvennye idei dekabristov* (Saint Petersburg: Tipografiia Pervoi Spb. Trudovoi Arteli, 1909), esp. pp. 507 ff.

8. The intriguing distinction between rationalism and nationalism was developed by L. Schapiro. See his *Rationalism and Nationalism in Russian Nineteenth-Century Political Thought* (New Haven: Yale University Press, 1967).

9. See M. Karpovich, "A Forerunner of Lenin: P. N. Tkachev," *Review of Politics*, vol. 6 (July 1944), pp. 336–49, and Rolf H. W. Theen, "The Idea of the Revolutionary State: Tkachev, Trotsky, and Lenin," *The Russian Review*, vol. 31, no. 3 (October 1972). On the concept of the "dictatorship of the proletariat" in Russian political thought, see the excellent essay by Darrell P. Hammer, "The Dictatorship of the Proletariat," in B. W. Eissenstat, ed., *Lenin and Leninism: State, Law, and Society* (Lexington, Mass.: Lexington Books, 1971), pp. 25–42.

10. M. P. Golubeva, "Moia pervaia vstrecha s Vladimirom Il'ichem," in *Vosp.* (1956), p. 113.

11. V. Bonch-Bruevich, "Biblioteka i arkhiv RSDRP v Zheneve," *Krasnaia letopis'*, no. 3 (48), (1932), pp. 113, 115.

12. On this point, see the excellent essay by Richard Pipes, "The Origins of Bolshevism: The Intellectual Evolution of Young Lenin," *op. cit.*, pp. 35–37.

13. P. N. Tkachev, *Izbrannye sochineniia na sotsial'no-politicheskie temy* (Moscow: Izdatel'stvo Vsesoiuznogo obshchestva politkatorzhan i ssyl'no-poselentsev, 1932), Vol. I, p. 70 (originally published in *Russkoe Slovo*, no. 12 (1865), in a review of a book by Iu. Zhukovskii).

14. See A. I. Ivanskii, comp., *Zhizn' kak fakel: Istoriia geroicheskoi bor'by i tragicheskoi gibeli Aleksandra Ul'ianova, rasskazannaia ego sovremennikami* (Moscow: Izdatel'stvo politicheskoi literatury, 1966), pp. 294 ff.; B. S. Itenberg and A. Ia. Cherniak, *Zhizn' Aleksandra Ul'ianova* (Moscow: Izdatel'stvo "Nauka," 1966), pp. 119 ff.; and Volin, *op. cit.*, p. 33.

15. A. A. Shilov, comp., *l marta 1887 g. Delo P. Shevyreva, A. Ul'ianova . . . i dr.* (Moscow-Leningrad: Moskovskii Rabochii, 1927), p. 377.

16. O. M. Govorukhin, "Vospominaniia o terroristicheskoi gruppe Aleksandra Il'icha Ul'ianova," *Oktiabr'*, no. 3 (1927), p. 134, and Ivanskii, *Zhizn' kak fakel*, p. 283.

17. Cf. K. Marks, *Vvedenie k kritike filosofii prava Gegelia. S. predisloviem P. L. Lavrova.* (Geneva: Vol'naia russkaia tipografiia, 1887). Anna Ulyanova's claim to have checked and corrected the translation (Ivanskii, *Zhizn' kak*

fakel, p. 284), is difficult to reconcile with the fact that she was unaware of her brother's involvement in the revolutionary movement when he was arrested. If she actually read the essay by Marx, she should have suspected that her brother had become a revolutionary.

18. Robert C. Tucker, ed., *The Marx-Engels Reader* (New York: Norton, 1972), p. 11.

19. See Rolf H. W. Theen, "Seizure of Political Power as the Prologue to Social Revolution: The Political Ideas of P. N. Tkachev in the Early 1870's," *Canadian Slavic Studies*, Vol. IV, no. 4 (Winter 1970), pp. 677–79.

20. See K. Marx, "Zur Kritik der Hegelschen Rechtsphilosophie. Einleitung," in Karl Marx and Friedrich Engels, *Werke* (Berlin: Dietz Verlag, 1970), vol. 1, esp. pp. 380, 382, 385–86, 388, and 390–91.

21. Cf. V. E. Postnikov, *Iuzhno-russkoe krest'ianskoe khoziaistvo* (Moscow, 1891). Apparently Lenin delivered a summary of the book sometime in the fall of 1892. See M. I. Semenov (M. Blan), *Revoliutsionnaia Samara 80–90–kh godov* (*Vospominaniia*) ([Kuibyshev]: Kuibyshevskoe izdatel'stvo, 1940), p. 65. Lenin also wrote an extensive review of the book and left marginal notes. See *PSS*, Vol. 1, pp. 3–66 and 537–46.

22. Valentinov, *The Early Years of Lenin*, pp. 159 ff. The notable exception is the above-cited essay by Richard Pipes.

23. Letter to P. P. Maslov, written in late December, 1893. See *PSS*, vol. 46, p. 2.

24. See *Perepiska K. Marksa i F. Engel'sa s russkimi politicheskimi deiateliami* (Leningrad: Gosudarstvennoe izdatel'stvo politicheskoi literatury, 1951), pp. 299 ff. Both Marx and Engels remained deliberately vague and ambivalent on the questions of central concern to the Russian revolutionaries, i.e., the fate of the village commune (*obshchina*), the possibility of a separate path to socialism, etc.

25. Lenin, *PSS*, Vol. 1, pp. 97, 105. See also his letter to Maslov, written in December of 1893, in which he takes the position that the workers do not constitute a separate class, but merely "the upper layers of that enormous mass

of the peasantry which already now lives by the sale of its labor power." (*Ibid.*, vol. 46, pp. 1–2.)

26. *Ibid.*, vol. 1, p. 280.

27. *Ibid.*, p. 312.

28. Ten years later Lenin explicitly referred to the early writings of Marx, published in four volumes by Franz Mehring under the title *Aus dem literarischen Nachlass von Karl Marx, Friedrich Engels, und Ferdinand Lassalle* (Stuttgart: Verlag von J. H. W. Dietz Nachf., 1902), in justifying his Jacobin position. See Lenin, *PSS*, vol. 11, pp. 47, 121.

29. M. Golubeva, "Poslednii karaul," pp. 30–31, and, by the same author, "Iunosha Ul'ianov (V. I. Lenin)," *Staryi Bol'shevik*, no. 5/8 (1933), pp. 162–63.

30. See R. H. McNeal, *Bride of the Revolution: Krupskaya and Lenin* (Ann Arbor: University of Michigan Press, 1972).

31. Richard Pipes, *Struve: Liberal on the Left, 1870–1905* (Cambridge: Harvard University Press, 1970), pp. 125 ff.; Valentinov, "Vstrecha Lenina s marksizmom," and, by the same author, "Iz proshlogo: P. B. Struve o Lenine," *Sotsialisticheskii Vestnik*, no. 8/9 (673–74), (1954), pp. 169–72. Fedoseev reportedly advised Lenin to tone down his criticism of Struve and may also have induced him to abandon—temporarily—the idea that capitalism was already a fact of Russian life. In any case, as early as 1894 Fedoseev had drawn a clear distinction between "primary capitalist accumulation" and "capitalism." See N. Fedoseev, *Stat'i i pis'ma* (Moscow: Gosudarstvennoe izdatel'stvo politicheskoi literatury, 1958), p. 126.

32. Lenin, *PSS*, vol. 2, pp. 84–85.

33. See *Zadachi russkikh sotsial-demokratov*, written in 1897, in *ibid.*, p. 450.

34. On Lenin's relationship to Krupskaya, cf. McNeal, *op. cit.*; for information on Lenin's relationship to Inessa Armand, see Bertram D. Wolfe, "Lenin and Inessa Armand," *Slavic Review*, no. 1 (1963), pp. 96–114, and by the same author, *Strange Communists I Have Known* (London–New York: George Allen and Unwin, 1965), pp. 138–64. Lenin's reaction to Inessa's death is described in Angelica Balabanoff,

Impressions of Lenin (Ann Arbor: University of Michigan Press, 1968), pp. 14–15.

35. Pipes, *Struve: Liberal on the Left, 1870–1905,* pp. 212 ff.

36. See, for example, his letter to A. N. Potresov, dated June 27, 1899, in *PSS*, vol. 46, pp. 32–33, and Martov's recollections in *Zapiski sotsial-demokrata* (Moscow: Krasnaia Nov', 1924), pp. 400 ff.

37. The author of this document was E. Kuskova, an exponent of "economism." The name "*Credo*," under which this statement of economist principles became known and famous, has been traced back to Lenin's sister Anna.

38. N. K. Krupskaia, "Iz vospominanii o V. I. Lenine," in *Vosp.* (1956), p. 105. On Lenin's reaction to Bernstein, see *PSS*, vol. 55, pp. 175–76. Lenin's violent reaction to Kuskova's *Credo* is evident in his "Protest rossiiskikh sotsial-demokratov," in *ibid.*, vol. 4, pp. 165–76.

39. *Ibid.*, pp. 193–94.

40. *Ibid.*, pp. 373–76.

41. *Lenin: Leben und Werk* (Vienna: Verlag für Kultur und Politik, 1924), p. 46.

CHAPTER 4

1. Lenin, *PSS*, vol. 4, p. 386.

2. See, for example, Lenin's letter to Plekhanov, dated January 1, 1901, in *ibid.*, vol. 46, p. 79. The essay attacking liberalism, whose language Lenin toned down as a concession to Akselrod and Plekhanov, was first published in December 1901 in *Zaria*. See *PSS*, vol. 5, pp. 21–72.

3. *Ibid.*, vol. 4, pp. 371–77.

4. See Lenin's letter to his sister Anna, dated April 8, 1909, in *ibid.*, vol. 55, p. 289.

5. Cf. "*Proekt i ob"iasnenie programmy sotsial-demokraticheskoi partii*," (1895–96), in *ibid.*, vol. 2, pp. 104, 101.

6. *Ibid.*, vol. 4, p. 377. After 1900 Lenin increasingly used military metaphors to describe the revolutionary struggle.

7. Cf. "How the 'Spark' Was Nearly Extinguished," in *PSS*, vol. 4, especially pp. 343–44. See also the excellent study by Dietrich Geyer, *Lenin in der russischen Sozialdemokratie* (Cologne: Böhlau-Verlag, 1962), pp. 187 ff.

8. While the significance of *What Is to Be Done?* is recognized by most scholars, some have denied its special importance or wider significance. See, for example, Meyer, *op. cit.*, and John Plamenatz, *German Marxism and Russian Communism* (New York: Longmans Green, 1954).

9. George Lukács, *Lenin: A Study on the Unity of His Thought* (Cambridge: MIT Press, 1971), p. 99.

10. See, for example, his letter to Plekhanov, in *PSS*, vol. 46, p. 186.

11. Eventually Lenin came to regard himself as one of the few real Socialists and as the first Marxist in fifty years who understood Marx. Cf. his *Philosophical Notebooks* of the year 1914, in *ibid.*, vol. 29, p. 162.

12. *Ulam, op. cit.*, p. 178.

13. Lenin, *PSS*, vol. 6, pp. 30, 38–39, 79.

14. *Ibid.*, pp. 31, 171–72.

15. *Ibid.*, pp. 52, 28, 74, 86, 77.

16. *Ibid.*, vol. 4, p. 183.

17. *Ibid.*, vol. 6, pp. 22, 9, 24.

18. *Ibid.*, pp. 80, 99, 107, 86, 69, 24–28.

19. See P. Tcatschoff, *Offener Brief an Herrn Friedrich Engels* (Zurich: Typographie der Tagwacht, 1874).

20. Lenin, *PSS*, vol. 6, pp. 25, 137–40, 127, 106, 25, and 135.

21. *Ibid.*, p. 164.

22. N. Trotskii, *Nashi politicheskie zadachi* (Geneva: Izdanie Rossiiskoi Sotsial'demokraticheskoi Rabochei Partii, 1904), especially pp. 90 ff.

23. Cf. N. K. Takhtarev, "V. I. Lenin i sotsial-demokraticheskoe dvizhenie," *Byloe*, no. 24 (1924), p. 22. On the revealing history of Lenin's relationship to Struve, see Pipes, *Struve: Liberal on the Left*, especially pp. 237 ff.

24. Lenin, *PSS*, vol. 42, pp. 71–72, and Branko Lazitch and Milorad M. Drachkovitch, *Lenin and the Comintern* (Stanford: Hoover Institution Press, 1972), Vol. I, pp. 544–45.

25. Literally translated "churchification" (German: *Ver-*

kirchlichung), i.e., the idea of transforming secular political power into ecclesiastical dominion.

26. For a more detailed analysis of the concept of the revolutionary state in Russian political thought, see Theen, "The Idea of the Revolutionary State: Tkachev, Trotsky, and Lenin." *The Russian Review*, vol. 31, no. 4 (October 1972), pp. 383 ff.

27. L. Trotsky, *The Permanent Revolution and Results and Prospects* (New York: Merit Publishers, 1969), p. 62.

28. V. I. Lenin, *The State and Revolution*, in *PSS*, vol. 33, pp. 28, 31, 88.

29. Karl Marx and Friedrich Engels, *Manifest der Kommunistischen Partei* (London: Office der Bildungs-Gesellschaft für Arbeiter, 1848), p. 15.

30. Cf., for example, the following revealing statement, written in 1902: "If we really *positively* knew that the petty bourgeoisie would support the proletariat at the time the latter achieved its proletarian revolution, then there would be no need to talk about 'dictatorship,' because then we would be guaranteed such an overwhelming majority that we could do beautifully without a dictatorship" (Lenin, *PSS*, vol. 6, p. 229).

31. *Ibid.*, vol. 33, p. 26.

32. *Ibid.*

33. Cf. Louis Fischer, *The Life of Lenin*, p. 122; R. V. Daniels, "The State and Revolution: A Case Study in the Genesis and Transformation of Communist Ideology," *American Slavic and East European Review*, vol. 12, no. 1 (February 1953), p. 22; and L. Schapiro, "Lenin After Fifty Years," *op. cit.*, p. 10.

34. For a detailed analysis of Lenin's utopianism, cf. Rodney Barfield, "Lenin's Utopianism: *State and Revolution*," *Slavic Review*, vol. 30, no. 1 (March 1971), pp. 45–56.

35. See Lenin's lecture on the 1905 Revolution, delivered on January 9 (22), 1917, in Zurich, in *PSS*, vol. 30, p. 328.

36. Cf. Lenin's letters to A. M. Kollontai, dated February 17, 1917, and to L. B. Kamenev, dated sometime between July 5 (18), and July 7 (20), 1917, in *ibid.*, vol. 48,

pp. 388, 444. The pamphlet was written in August and September of 1917 and published in 1918 without essential changes.

37. *Ibid.*, vol. 33, pp. 96–97.

CHAPTER 5

1. Lenin, *PSS*, vol. 33, p. 120.

2. *Ibid.*, vol. 11, p. 103.

3. *Ibid.*, vol. 30, p. 311.

4. W. H. Chamberlin, *The Russian Revolution* (New York: Grosset & Dunlap, 1965), Vol. I, pp. 118–19.

5. Lenin, *PSS*, vol. 44, p. 197.

6. See "Vypiski i zamechaniia na knigu Klauzevitsa 'O voine i vedenii voin," *Leninskii sbornik*, Vol. XII (1930), p. 412. These excerpts and notes were not included in the fifth and most complete edition of Lenin's works published to date. For a detailed analysis of the influence of von Clausewitz on Lenin, see Werner Hahlweg, "Lenin und Clausewitz," *Archiv für Kulturgeschichte*, vol. 36 (1954), pp. 30–59, 357–87.

7. Leon Trotsky, *My Life* (New York: Grosset & Dunlap, 1960), p. 337, and *Lenin* (New York: Capricorn Books, 1962), p. 102.

8. V. I. Lenin, *Sochineniia* (Moscow-Leningrad: Partizdat TsK VKP (b), 1929), 3rd ed., vol. 22, pp. 36–37.

9. Lenin, *PSS*, vol. 35, pp. 19, 27.

10. The Mensheviks won 16 seats; the Constitutional Democrats or Kadets 17; various nationality groups 86; and miscellaneous organizations the remaining 3 seats. On the Constituent Assembly, cf. O. H. Radkey, *The Elections to the Russian Constituent Assembly of 1917* (Cambridge: Harvard University Press, 1950).

11. See "Neskol'ko tesizov," published in *Sotsial-Demokrat*, no. 47 (October 13, 1915), in Lenin, *PSS*, vol. 27, p. 50.

12. See, for example, *Protokoly Tsentral'nogo Komiteta RSDRP* (Moscow, 1929), pp. 201, 292.

13. During Lenin's lifetime, the Bolshevik Party was

always very much of an elite party. With a population of 163 million in Russia in 1917, the Bolshevik Party had only 24,000 members at the time of the Revolution. In 1918 its membership stood at 390,000. It decreased to 350,000 in 1919, increased to 611,978 in 1920 and 732,521 in 1921, only to decrease once again to 528,354 in 1922, 499,100 in 1923, and 472,000 in 1924. See T. H. Rigby, *Communist Party Membership in the U.S.S.R., 1917–1967* (Princeton: Princeton University Press, 1968), p. 52.

14. Lenin, *PSS*, vol. 33, pp. 35, 56.

15. *Ibid.*, pp. 65, 89.

16. *Ibid.*, p. 95.

17. *Ibid.*, vol. 35, p. 66.

18. See *ibid.*, vol. 33, pp. 59, 35; vol. 36, p. 205; vol. 38, p. 325.

19. *Ibid.*, vol. 33, p. 29.

20. Pasternak, *Dr. Zhivago*, p. 378.

21. Lenin, *PSS*, vol. 35, p. 273.

22. *Ibid.*, vol. 36, pp. 65–66.

23. *Ibid.*, vol. 39, pp. 73, 84. The text of the second lecture, delivered on August 29, 1919, has apparently been lost. See V. I. Lenin, *Sochineniia* ([Moscow], 1935), 3rd ed., vol. 24, p. 787.

24. *Ibid.*, vol. 40, pp. 207, 208.

25. *Ibid.*, vol. 43, p. 57. Articles advocating the NEP appeared in *Pravda* as early as February 17 and 26, 1921. On February 24 a detailed draft of Lenin's proposals was submitted to the Central Committee and approved, in revised form, on March 7, 1921. On March 8 Lenin cautiously outlined his proposals in his general policy speech at the Tenth Party Congress. (See *ibid.*, pp. 7 ff.)

26. *Ibid.*, p. 13.

27. Lenin himself seems to have given the signal for the repression of the Mensheviks in May of 1921, in a pamphlet written to explain the "new [economic] policy and its conditions." Non-party people, Lenin wrote, "who are nothing else but Mensheviks and SRs dressed in modern, Kronstadt-non-party attire," should be kept "parsimoniously in prison or sent to Martov in Berlin for the free enjoyment

of all the amenities of genuine democracy." (*Ibid.*, pp. 244–45)

28. Letter dated May 16, 1921, in *ibid.*, vol. 52, pp. 193–94.

29. *Ibid.*, vol. 44, pp. 364, 366.

30. Letters of February 20 and 21, 1921, in *ibid.*, pp. 367, 368–69.

31. *Ibid.*, vol. 45, pp. 360–62.

32. *Ibid.*, p. 362.

33. Alexander Herzen, *Selected Philosophical Works* (Moscow: Foreign Languages Publishing House, 1956), p. 473.

34. Antecedents of this "Eastern orientation" of Lenin's Marxism can be found in his earlier writings, especially in his theory of imperialism. However, until the Bolshevik hopes of an imminent revolution in Western Europe were disappointed, Leninism remained in many respects a Western-oriented theory of revolution. The explicit Eastern orientation is characteristic of Lenin's thinking in late 1922 and 1923.

35. On the relationship between the concepts of *Selbstentfremdung*, i.e., self-alienation, and *Klassenkampf*, i.e., class struggle, in the thought of Marx, see Robert C. Tucker, *Philosophy and Myth in Karl Marx* (New York: Cambridge University Press, 1961), especially pp. 165 ff.

36. Lenin, *PSS*, vol. 45, p. 404.

37. *Ibid.*, pp. 402–4.

38. This information is based on the recollections of Boris I. Nicolaevsky, who had a series of conversations with Bukharin in 1936 in Paris. See "An Interview with Boris Nicolaevsky," in Boris I. Nicolaevsky, *Power and the Soviet Elite* (New York: Frederick A. Praeger, 1965), p. 12.

39. Lenin, *PSS*, vol. 45, pp. 372, 376, 389.

40. *Ibid.*, pp. 383, 392.

41. Lenin, *PSS*, vol. 41, p. 383.

42. Roy A. Medvedev, *Let History Judge: The Origins and Consequences of Stalinism*. Trans. Colleen Taylor. Ed. David Joravsky and Georges Haupt. (New York: Alfred A. Knopf, 1972), pp. 16–18.

43. Cf. N. Valentinov (Vol'skii), *Novaia ekonomicheskaia politika i krizis partii posle smerti Lenina. Gody raboty v VSNKH vo vremia NEP. Vospominaniia*, ed. J. Bunyan and V. Butenko, with an introduction by Bertram Wolfe (Stanford: Hoover Institution Press, 1971), p. 185.

44. F. M. Dostoevskii, *Polnoe sobranie khudozhestvennykh proizvedenii* (Moscow-Leningrad: Gosudarstvennoe izdatel'stvo, 1927), Vol. VII, p. 329. Fyodor Dostoyevsky, *The Possessed*, trans. Constance Garnett (New York: The Modern Library, 1963), p. 409.

SELECTED BIBLIOGRAPHY

回 回 回

Balabanoff, Angelica, *Impressions of Lenin*. Translated by Isotta Cesari. Foreword by Bertram Wolfe. (Ann Arbor: The University of Michigan Press, 1968).

Browder, R. P., and Kerensky, A. F., eds., *The Russian Provisional Government, 1917: Documents* (Stanford: Stanford University Press, 1961), 3 vols.

Chamberlin, W. H., *The Russian Revolution* (New York: Grosset & Dunlap, 1965), 2 vols.

Deutscher, Isaac, *Lenin's Childhood* (London: Oxford University Press, 1970).

Eissenstadt, B. W., ed., *Lenin and Leninism* (Lexington: Lexington Books, 1971).

Elizarova, A. I., "Vospominaniia ob Aleksandre Il'iche Ul'ianove," *Proletarskaia revoliutsiia*, no. 1 (60), (1927), pp. 70–124; no. 2–3 (61–62), (1927), pp. 278–316.

Fischer, Louis, *The Life of Lenin* (New York: Harper & Row, 1964).

Fotieva, L. A., *Iz vospominanii o V. I. Lenine* (*Dekabr' 1922–Mart 1923 g.*) (Moscow: Izdatel'stvo politicheskoi literatury, 1964).

———, *Iz zhizni V. I. Lenina* (Moscow: Izdatel'stvo politicheskoi literatury, 1967).

Geyer, Dietrich, *Lenin in der russischen Sozialdemokratie* (Cologne: Böhlau-Verlag, 1962).

Golubeva, M., "Iunosha Ul'ianov (V. I. Lenin)," *Staryi Bol'shevik*, no. 5/8 (1933), pp. 160–64.

———, "Poslednii karaul," *Molodaia gvardiia*, no. 2–3 (1924), pp. 29–31.

Gorkii, M., "Vladimir Lenin," *Russkii sovremennik*, no. 1 (1924), pp. 229–44.

Gorky, M., *Days with Lenin* (New York: International Publishers, 1932).

Hahlweg, W., *Lenins Rückkehr nach Russland 1917* (Leiden: E. J. Brill, 1957).

Haimson, L. H., *The Russian Marxists and the Origins of Bolshevism* (Cambridge: Harvard University Press, 1955).

Ivanskii, A., ed., *Molodoi Lenin: Povest' v dokumentakh i memuarakh* (Moscow: Izdatel'stvo politicheskoi literatury, 1964).

Khronologicheskii ukazatel' proizvedenii V. I. Lenina (Moscow: Gosudarstvennoe izdatel'stvo politicheskoi literatury, 1959–62), 2 vols.

Krupskaya, N. K., *Memories of Lenin (1893–1917)* (London: Lawrence and Wishart, 1942).

Lalaiants, I., "O moikh vstrechakh s V. I. Leninym za vremia 1893–1900 gg.," *Proletarskaia revoliutsiia*, no. 1 (84), (1929), pp. 38–70.

Lenin, V. I., *Collected Works* (Moscow: Foreign Languages Publishing House, 1960–68), 40 vols. (Translated from the 4th and 5th Russian editions).

————, *Polnoe sobranie sochinenii* (Moscow: Gosudarstvennoe izdatel'stvo politicheskoi literatury, 1958–65), 55 vols. and index.

————, *Sochineniia* (Moscow-Leningrad: Partizdat TsK VKP (b), 1935), 3rd ed., 30 vols. and index.

————, "Vypiski i zamechaniia na knigu Klauzevitsa 'O voine i vedenii voin,'" *Leninskii sbornik*, Vol. XII (1930), pp. 387–452.

Leninskii sbornik (Moscow: Imprint varies, 1924–59), 36 vols.

Lewin, Moshe, *Lenin's Last Struggle* (New York: Vintage Books, 1970).

Luxemburg, Rosa, *The Russian Revolution*. Introduction by Bertram D. Wolfe. (New York: Workers Age Publishers, 1940).

McNeal, R. H., *Bride of the Revolution: Krupskaya and Lenin* (Ann Arbor: The University of Michigan Press, 1972).

Martov, Iu., *Zapiski sotsial-demokrata* (Moscow: Krasnaia Nov', 1924).

Medvedev, Roy A., *Let History Judge: The Origins and Consequences of Stalinism*. Trans. by Colleen Taylor. Ed. by David Joravsky and Georges Haupt. (New York: Alfred A. Knopf, 1972).

Meyer, A., *Leninism* (Cambridge: Harvard University Press, 1957).

Perepiska sem'i Ul'ianovykh, 1883–1917 (Moscow: Izdatel'stvo politicheskoi literatury, 1969).

Pipes, Richard, "The Origins of Bolshevism: The Intellectual Evolution of Young Lenin," in R. Pipes, ed., *Revolutionary Russia* (Cambridge: Harvard University Press, 1968), pp. 26–62.

———, "Russian Marxism and Its Populist Background," *The Russian Review*, vol. 19, no. 4 (October 1960), pp. 316–37.

———, *Social Democracy and the St. Petersburg Labor Movement, 1885–1897* (Cambridge: Harvard University Press, 1963).

———, *Struve: Liberal on the Left, 1870–1905* (Cambridge: Harvard University Press, 1970).

Plamenatz, John, *German Marxism and Russian Communism* (New York: Longmans Green, 1954).

Polevoi, Iu. Z., *Zarozhdenie marksizma v Rossii 1883–1894 gg.* (Moscow: Izdatel'stvo Akademii Nauk SSSR, 1959).

Pospelov, P. N., *et al.*, ed., *Vladimir Il'ich Lenin. Biografiia.* (Moscow: Gosudarstvennoe izdatel'stvo politicheskoi literatury, 1960).

Possony, S. T., *Lenin: The Compulsive Revolutionary* (Chicago: Henry Regnery Company, 1964).

Rauch, Georg von, *Lenin: Die Grundlegung des Sowjetsystems* (Berlin: Musterschmidt-Verlag, 1962).

Reminiscences of Lenin by His Relatives (Moscow: Foreign Languages Publishing House, 1956).

Schapiro, Leonard, *The Communist Party of the Soviet Union* (New York: Random House, 1960).

———, *The Origin of the Communist Autocracy: Political Opposition in the Soviet State: First Phase, 1917–1922.* (Cambridge: Harvard University Press, 1955).

———, *Rationalism and Nationalism in Russian Nineteenth-Century Political Thought* (New Haven: Yale University Press, 1967).

———, and Reddaway, P., eds., *Lenin: The Man, the Theorist, the Leader* (New York: Frederick A. Praeger, 1968).

Scheibert, Peter, "Über Lenins Anfänge," *Historische Zeitschrift*, no. 182 (1956), pp. 549–66.

———, *Von Bakunin zu Lenin* (Leiden: E. J. Brill, 1956), Vol. I.

Shaginian, Marietta, *Bilet po istorii* (Sem'ia Ul'ianovykh). Roman. Chast' I. (Moscow: Gosudarstvennoe izdatel'stvo "Khudozhestvennaia literatura," 1938).

———, "Predki Lenina," *Novyi mir*, no. 11 (November 1937), pp. 262–85.

Shub, David, *Lenin* (Garden City: Doubleday & Company, 1948).

Thiesen, A. U., *Lenins politische Ethik nach den Prinzipien seiner politischen Doktrin* (Munich: Verlag Anton Pustet, 1965).

Trotsky, L., *Lenin* (New York: Capricorn Books, 1962).

———, *My Life* (New York: Grosset & Dunlap, 1960).

Trotsky, Leon, *The Young Lenin.* Translation and Introduction by Max Eastman (Garden City: Doubleday & Company, 1972).

Trotzki, Leo, *Der junge Lenin*. Translated by Walter Fischer. (Vienna: Verlag Fritz Molden, 1969).

Tucker, Robert C., *The Marxian Revolutionary Idea* (New York: W. W. Norton & Company, 1969).

Ulam, Adam B., *The Bolsheviks* (New York: The Macmillan Company, 1965).

Valentinov, N., *Encounters with Lenin*. Translated by Paul Rosta and Brian Pearce. Foreword by Leonard Schapiro. (London: Oxford University Press, 1968).

———, *The Early Years of Lenin*. Translated and edited by Rolf H. W. Theen. Introduction by Bertram D. Wolfe. (Ann Arbor: The University of Michigan Press, 1969).

Venturi, Franco, *Roots of Revolution* (New York: Alfred A. Knopf, 1960).

Vladimir Il'ich Lenin. Biograficheskaia khronika. (Moscow: Izdatel'stvo politicheskoi literatury, 1970–71), 2 vols.

Volin, B., *Lenin v Povolzh'e 1870–1893* (Moscow: Gosudarstvennoe izdatel'stvo politicheskoi literatury, 1956).

Vospominaniia o Vladimire Il'iche Lenine (Moscow: Gosudarstvennoe izdatel'stvo politicheskoi literatury, 1956–61), 3 vols.

Vospominaniia o Vladimire Il'iche Lenine (Moscow: Gosudarstvennoe izdatel'stvo politicheskoi literatury, 1969–70), 5 vols.

Walter, Gérard, *Lénine* (Paris: Julliard, 1950).

Wilson, Edmund, *To the Finland Station* (Garden City: Doubleday & Company, 1940).

Wolfe, Bertram D., *An Ideology in Power: Reflections on the Russian Revolution* (New York: Stein and Day, 1969).

———, "Leninism," in Milorad Drachkovitch, ed., *Marxism in the Modern World* (Stanford: Hoover Institution on War, Revolution, and Peace, 1965), pp. 47–89.

———, *Three Who Made a Revolution* (Boston: Beacon Press, 1962).

Wolfenstein, E. Victor, *The Revolutionary Personality: Lenin, Trotsky, Gandhi* (Princeton: Princeton University Press, 1967).

Yarmolinsky, Avrahm, *Road to Revolution: A Century of Russian Radicalism* (New York: Collier Books, 1962).

Zetkin, Klara, *Reminiscences of Lenin* (London: Modern Books Limited, 1929).

DATE DUE